NEVER TO RETURN

BRIGHTON COLLEGE'S FALLEN 1914–1918

MAX USHER

Published in Great Britain in 2016 by Shire Publications (part of Bloomsbury Publishing Plc), PO Box 883, Oxford, OX1 9PL, UK.

1385 Broadway, 5th Floor New York, NY 10018, USA.

E-mail: shire@shirebooks.co.uk   www.shirebooks.co.uk

SHIRE is a trademark of Osprey Publishing, a division of Bloomsbury Publishing Plc.

A CIP catalogue record for this book is available from the British Library.

ISBN-13: 978 1 78442 157 1
PDF e-book ISBN: 978 1 78442 159 5
ePub ISBN: 978 1 78442 158 8

Brighton College has asserted its right under the Copyright, Designs and Patents Act, 1988, to be identified as the author of this book.

Typeset in Garamond Premier Pro, Sabon and Candara

Printed in Slovenia by Global Printing Solutions Group.

16 17 18 19 20   10 9 8 7 6 5 4 3 2 1

COVER IMAGE:
Brighton College Centennial Remembrance Statue by Philip Jackson CVO DL MA FBRS. (Photograph by Daniel Shearing)

TITLE PAGE IMAGE:
Illustration of the Brighton College gateway by Anthony Hill.

CONTENTS PAGE IMAGE:
Memorial to Captain Gilbert Maurice Parkinson, in Brighton College Chapel see page 150.

ABBREVIATIONS USED IN TEXT:
AIF: Australian Imperial Force
ANZAC: Australian and New Zealand Army Corps
BEF: British Expeditionary Force
CEF: Canadian Expeditionary Force
DSO: Distinguished Service Order
HAC: Honourable Artillery Company
MC: Military Cross
MO: Medical Officer
OB: Old Brightonian
OTC: Officers' Training Corps
RAF: Royal Air Force
RAMC: Royal Army Medical Corps
RFA: Royal Field Artillery
RFC: Royal Flying Corps
RGA: Royal Garrison Artillery
RMA: Royal Military Academy
RMC: Royal Military College
RNAS: Royal Naval Air Service

BRIGHTON COLLEGE:
Brighton College is a registered charity, number 307061. Brighton College, Eastern Road, Brighton, East Sussex, BN2 0AL. www.brightoncollege.org.uk

Contents

HE LEFT THIS PLACE
NEVER TO RETURN

BE GRATEFUL

Roll of Honour

NAME	CAUSE OF DEATH	DATE OF DEATH	PLACE	AGE
Vincent Waterfall	Killed in action	22 August 1914	Belgium	22
John Whish	Died of wounds	8 September 1914	France	37
Geoffrey White	Killed in action	10 September 1914	Belgium	23
Neil Wright	Killed in action	15 September 1914	France	20
Paul Veyrier-Montagnères	Killed in action	18 September 1914	France	23
Hargrave Curtis-Raleigh	Died of illness	27 September 1914	India	29
Rodolphe Armbruster	Killed in action	23 October 1914	France	21
Charles King	Killed in action	30 October 1914	Belgium	51
Harley Duff	Killed in action	1 November 1914	Belgium	18
Ernest Lane-Anderson	Killed in action	10 November 1914	Belgium	20
Lionel Gaisford	Died of wounds	23 November 1914	France	26
Reginald Pope	Killed in action	16 February 1915	Belgium	23
William Coxon	Killed in action	11 March 1915	France	21
Henry Etlinger	Died of wounds	27 April 1915	Belgium	35
Edward Baddeley	Killed in action	8 May 1915	Belgium	38
Leonard Walford	Killed in action	8 May 1915	Belgium	19
Val Lander	Killed in action	9 May 1915	France	21
Isaac Ridgway	Died of wounds	12 May 1915	Turkey	28
Gordon Belcher	Killed in action	16 May 1915	Belgium	29
Albert Holmes	Died of pneumonia	19 May 1915	Great Britain	43
John Stollery	Killed in action	24 May 1915	Belgium	28
Eric Garner-Smith	Killed in action	25 May 1915	France	23
Frank Keddell	Killed in action	8 June 1915	France	23
Henry Hatton	Killed in action	16 June 1915	Belgium	28
John Wickham	Died of wounds	22 June 1915	Belgium	30
Hubert Nunn	Killed in action	23 June 1915	Turkey	24
Edward Dyer	Killed in action	28 June 1915	Turkey	41
Alexander Glenday	Died of wounds	8 August 1915	France	27
Aubrey Fyldes	Killed in action	9 August 1915	Turkey	18
Philip Williams	Killed in action	10 August 1915	Turkey	21
Henry Watkin	Died of wounds	21 August 1915	Turkey	41
Dennis Blyth	Killed in action	28 August 1915	Belgium	22
Walter Martin	Killed in action	13 September 1915	France	22
Alan Ventris	Killed in action	14 September 1915	Belgium	18
Alan Young	Killed in action	25 September 1915	France	20

NAME	CAUSE OF DEATH	DATE OF DEATH	PLACE	AGE
Bryan Cubitt	Killed in action	26 September 1915	France	23
Kenneth Goodyear	Killed in action	28 September 1915	France	25
Edward Vaile	Killed in action	5 October 1915	Belgium	24
Walter Stewart	Died of wounds	3 November 1915	Great Britain	42
Herbert Lewis	Killed in action	4 November 1915	Turkey	20
Edward Welch	Killed in action	22 December 1915	Mesopotamia	26
Charles Turton	Accidentally killed	4 February 1916	Great Britain	21
Leslie Evans	Died of wounds	16 March 1916	Belgium	19
Reginald Reade	Killed in action	5 April 1916	Mesopotamia	24
Alfred Webb	Died of wounds	4 May 1916	Mesopotamia	22
Leslie Young	Killed in action	21 May 1916	France	25
William Griffith	Killed in action	31 May 1916	Battle of Jutland	18
Leslie Woodroffe	Died of wounds	4 June 1916	France	30
Hubert Garbett	Killed in action	30 June 1916	France	28
Basil Belcher	Killed in action	1 July 1916	France	22
George Guyon	Killed in action	1 July 1916	France	41
Spencer Jeudwine	Killed in action	1 July 1916	France	20
Gerald Neame	Killed in action	1 July 1916	France	31
Theodore Chalk	Killed in action	3 July 1916	France	30
Lister Wickham	Killed in action	3 July 1916	France	21
Gilfrid Reeve	Killed in action	8 July 1916	France	27
George Venner	Killed in action	8 July 1916	France	24
Ralph Wickham	Killed in action	9 July 1916	Belgium	41
John Scobie	Killed in action	29 July 1916	France	21
David Gaussen	Killed in action	31 July 1916	France	23
George Ross	Killed in action	9 August 1916	France	31
Maurice Frisch	Killed in action	25 August 1916	France	22
Charlton Reade	Killed in action	9 September 1916	France	18
Walter Bartlett	Killed in action	14 September 1916	France	38
John Webb	Killed in action	14 September 1916	France	21
Ferdinand Glenday	Killed in action	15 September 1916	France	24
John Mackreth	Killed in action	15 September 1916	France	23
Robert Mitchell	Killed in action	10 October 1916	Belgium	41
Herbert Sawyer	Killed in action	12 October 1916	France	27
Philip Vaile	Accidentally killed	14 October 1916	France	22
Frederick Brown	Killed in action	13 November 1916	France	25
Derrick Johnson	Killed in action	4 December 1916	France	21
Harold Body	Killed in action	15 December 1916	Belgium	26
Robert Odell	Died of wounds	20 December 1916	France	22
Harold Surgey	Killed in action	3 January 1917	East Africa	23
William Kemp	Killed in action	28 February 1917	France	20
John Buckland	Killed in action	1 March 1917	France	20
Ronald Ross	Killed in action	4 March 1917	France	21
Bertram Hazlehurst	Died of wounds	16 March 1917	France	20
Frederick Bartley	Killed in action	26 March 1917	Palestine	30
Sidney Stretton	Accidentally killed	27 March 1917	Great Britain	28
Alfred Schiff	Killed in action	9 April 1917	France	19

NAME	CAUSE OF DEATH	DATE OF DEATH	PLACE	AGE
Edmund Childe-Pemberton	Died of wounds	13 April 1917	France	21
Foster Thorne	Killed in action	18 April 1917	Mesopotamia	36
William Jay	Killed in action	25 April 1917	France	22
William Clapp	Died of wounds	29 April 1917	France	23
George Archdale	Died of wounds	30 April 1917	France	20
Leonard Gandar-Dower	Killed in action	3 May 1917	France	26
John Ainslie	Killed in action	19 May 1917	France	29
Francis Morris	Died of wounds	29 May 1917	France	21
Raymond Belemore	Died of wounds	8 June 1917	France	31
George Knowles	Died of wounds	10 June 1917	France	19
Arthur Hodge	Killed in action	13 June 1917	France	20
George Harvey	Killed in action	21 June 1917	France	38
Archer Richardson	Killed in action	25 June 1917	Belgium	24
Edgar Uridge	Killed in action	26 June 1917	France	20
Harold Belcher	Killed in action	8 July 1917	Belgium	42
John Akers	Killed in action	20 July 1917	Belgium	19
William Ross	Killed in action	23 July 1917	Belgium	25
Edward Nunn	Died of fever	24 July 1917	Mesopotamia	20
Colin Wise	Killed in action	31 July 1917	Belgium	25
Guy Hamilton	Killed in action	1 August 1917	Belgium	19
Eric Halliwell	Killed in action	11 September 1917	Belgium	20
William Botting	Killed in action	25 September 1917	Belgium	22
Bertram Kilner	Killed in action	25 September 1917	Over the North Sea	22
Bernard Powers	Killed in action	25 September 1917	France	20
Francis Thompson	Died of wounds	3 October 1917	Belgium	28
Leslie Scott	Killed in action	12 October 1917	Belgium	33
Hugo Bazett	Killed in action	14 October 1917	Belgium	38
Richard Groves	Died of wounds	24 October 1917	Belgium	20
Charles Homer	Accidentally killed while flying	27 October 1917	Great Britain	23
Harold Wright	Killed in action	30 October 1917	Belgium	27
Henry Griffith	Accidentally killed while flying	2 November 1917	Great Britain	26
Ewart Mackintosh	Killed in action	21 November 1917	France	24
Leonard Lee	Killed in action	30 November 1917	France	19
George Tolson	Died of wounds	1 December 1917	Palestine	28
Raymond Belcher	Died of wounds	7 December 1917	France	34
Robert Harvey	Killed in action	25 December 1917	France	22
Frederick Hobson	Killed in action	19 March 1918	Belgium	35
Roger King	Invalided from the army and died	19 March 1918	Great Britain	43
Eric Williams	Killed in action	27 March 1918	France	23
Geoffrey Neame	Killed in action	2 April 1918	France	34
George King	Died of wounds	30 April 1918	France	22
Egbert Hulbert	Killed in action	25 May 1918	France	19
Francis Butt	Killed in action	26 May 1918	France	18

NAME	CAUSE OF DEATH	DATE OF DEATH	PLACE	AGE
William Silver	Killed in action	8 June 1918	France	36
Roy Field	Died of wounds	29 June 1918	France	19
Robert Horton	Died of wounds	13 August 1918	France	20
Victor Bone	Killed in action	18 September 1918	Macedonia	21
Richard Norton	Killed in action	18 September 1918	France	19
William Price	Killed in action	21 September 1918	Palestine	28
Alfred Westwood	Killed in action	21 September 1918	France	28
Cyril West	Killed in action	28 September 1918	Belgium	19
Geoffrey Bonser	Killed in action	29 September 1918	Belgium	29
Frederic Hedgcock	Killed in action	29 September 1918	France	20
Colin Campbell	Died of wounds	30 September 1918	France	21
Charles Burt	Died of illness	27 October 1918	Ireland	32
Keith Scobie	Accidentally killed	27 October 1918	Great Britain	21
Nikolai de Plaoutine	Died of smallpox	31 October 1918	Poland/Ukraine	50
Herman Oxley	Killed in action	4 November 1918	France	25
Arthur Cave	Died of pneumonia	10 November 1918	Great Britain	22
Gilbert Parkinson	Died of pneumonia	14 November 1918	Italy	22
Reginald Grant	Unknown	26 November 1918	Great Britain	42
Sidney Pearce	Died of pneumonia	6 December 1918	Great Britain	28
Godfrey Thomas	Died of exhaustion	17 February 1919	Great Britain	62
John Burstall	Died of wounds	12 April 1919	France	42
Christopher Trafford	Died of tuberculosis	14 September 1919	Great Britain	19
Samuel Newton	Died of wounds	13 December 1919	Great Britain	22
Hector Crosley	Died of malaria contracted during military service	13 August 1921	Madeira	33

On page 5 and opposite: *Brighton College Centennial Remembrance Statue 2016, by Philip Jackson CVO DL MA FRBS.*

MICHAEL ALLEN (AGE 23)
WILLIAM BAILLIE (AGE 19)
LIONEL BAILY (AGE 21)
TRISTAN BALLANCE (AGE 27)
KONSTANTIN BALLAS-ANDERSEN (AGE 24)
JOHN BARDER (AGE 22)
ARTHUR BARKER (AGE 34)
JOHN BARTLETT (AGE 29)
MARTIN BAXTER-PHILLIPS (AGE 26)
RICHARD BAYLDON (AGE 26)
RAYMOND BELCHER (AGE 26)
JOHN BIGLAND (AGE 34)
ANTHONY BOWES (AGE 30)
ARCHIBALD BRANKSTON (AGE 31)
JOHN BRYDGES (AGE 28)
GILBERT BUCHANAN (AGE 36)
GEORGE BUXTON (AGE 21)
THOMAS CARTWRIGHT (AGE 25)
OWEN CHAVE (AGE 30)
AERNOUT VAN CITTERS (AGE 32)
DENNIS CLARK (AGE 30)
GERALD CLAYTON (AGE 23)
ANTHONY CLINCH (AGE 21)
PETER CLOSE (AGE 32)
HUGH COLBOURNE (AGE 17)
DESMOND COOKE (AGE 19)

MICHAEL DAWSON (AGE 31)
PAUL DAWSON (AGE 36)
JOHN DIXON (AGE 22)
STEPHEN DONOGHUE (AGE 21)
FRANK DUESBURY (AGE 22)
GEORGE DVORJETZ (AGE 25)
GORDON ELLIOTT (AGE 23)
RAYMOND ELLIOTT (AGE 22)
RICHARD ENGLAND (AGE 27)
LEONID EREMINSKY (AGE 22)
RICHARD FANSHAWE (AGE 35)
STANLEY FASE (AGE 22)
HENRY FEATHERSTONE (AGE 20)
JOHN FELLOWES (AGE 34)
JOHN FITCH (AGE 32)
JOHN FLEETWOOD (AGE 21)
ALFRED FLEMING (AGE 29)
HARRY FORD (AGE 35)
PAUL FRANKLIN (AGE 31)
GORDON FRASER (AGE 31)
GAVIN GALBRAITH (AGE 71)
DIMITRI GALITZINE (AGE 26)
PHILIP GIBBS (AGE 21)
SAMUEL GINN (AGE 32)
HECTOR GRAHAM (AGE 29)
CECIL GROVE (AGE 37)

Preface

This book is a memorial and a warning.

It is a memorial to the lives of 149 Brighton College pupils who lost all that they had to give. Here we catch glimpses of the schoolboys they once were. The cricketer. The actor. The school prefect. The recognised and the unrecognised. We get a sense of what they might have become. A lawyer. A vicar. A colonial administrator. And we learn something of their families. Parents. Brothers and sisters. Wives and children. In some cases we see pictures of their homes. An Edwardian terrace in Hove. A vicarage in Lincolnshire. A palace in St Petersburg. Each boy, each man, has his own story. Yet theirs was a common destiny. Death before their time. And it is about their deaths that we know most. We might argue about the virtues of the cause for which they died but we cannot argue with the virtue of their sacrifice. They died believing that they were defending our country, its values and its traditions. And for that, we owe thanks and respect.

But this book is also a warning. This island has been untouched by war for 71 years. We have grown accustomed to peace and we take it for granted. We cannot imagine a day when a whole generation will be called upon once again to make the ultimate sacrifice. But we must be vigilant. Freedom is not free.

Richard Cairns,
Head Master,
Brighton College,
July 2016

Above: *Richard Cairns, Remembrance Day Ceremony, 11 November 2014.*

THE CALL
1914
A Tribute

Introduction

The origins of this book lie in the 'Lest We Forget' project undertaken by all 214 members of the Brighton College Fourth Form in the academic year 2014–15. All were asked, together with their families, to research and write up a particular Old Brightonian killed in the First World War, using such resources as were available, for example the 1911 Census and the College's own reports and records. Many of the projects were excellent; others ran up against the problem familiar to historians of conflicting or incomplete information. Nonetheless, in their entirety the projects provide a substantial body of knowledge about the lives and deaths of those 149 Old Brightonians, whose names were listed in the College records but about whom very little else was known. Accordingly, the Head Master, Richard Cairns, asked me to use the projects to create a biographical guide to the names on the War Memorial outside the north door of the chapel. It should be added that the 149 listed there do not represent the sum total of the Brightonians who served in the Great War, indeed the total number was recorded as being 976, and that, furthermore, the school was much smaller than it is now, the annual roll in 1914 being 233. In that context the scale of the losses suffered and the commitment to the war effort made by pupils of the school is much larger than it might first appear and the need to record their lives and deaths much greater.

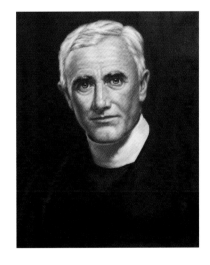

When investigating the lives of so many individuals it is inevitably easier to find out more about some than others. If, therefore, certain entries are occasionally surprisingly slender or couched in frustratingly conditional words such

Above: *Portrait of Canon W. R. Dawson by Finch, date unknown. In summer 1914 he addressed the school in Chapel, calling on every boy present to stand ready to sacrifice his life in defence of his country. Though the events that sparked the war had not yet unfolded, he clearly sensed the underlying volatility.*

Opposite: *Scottish American War Memorial in West Princes Street Gardens in Edinburgh. On the frieze at the back of the memorial are the words 'If it be life that waits I shall live forever unconquered; if death I shall die at last strong in my pride and free', from the poem 'The Creed' by Lt Ewart Mackintosh MC OB (1893–1917) (see page 125).*

EVERY POUND INVESTED IN
NATIONAL
WAR BONDS

MEANS
MORE SHIPS
MORE FOOD
AND
EARLIER VICTORY

N°65

as 'may', 'appears' or 'probably', please be assured that such entries are as frustrating, if not more so, to the author as they are to the reader. Faced by these obstacles, the Head Master and I agreed that it was better to include something about everyone, including those we were least sure about, than to exclude them altogether because it would be wrong to diminish the memory of those about whom less is known. Readers may also be surprised that a few of the 149 do not appear to have died while on active service, but instead due to either disease or accidental death. There was much debate about the inclusion of these individuals both on the memorial and in this book but it was eventually decided that the views of those who originally compiled the Roll of Honour in the early 1920s should be followed. It was their decision that all those on the Roll had died due to the war which they had collectively just endured and that an attempt to second guess the worthiness of those individuals from a distance of nearly a hundred years was not worthwhile.

Each entry begins with what could be ascertained about each OB's family background, including, where possible, place and date of birth, father's occupation, mother's maiden name and other details of family life. These details are followed by what is known of their school careers and early adult life before entry into the armed forces. Finding accurate and comprehensive information for this section was often the hardest part, both for the pupils undertaking the projects and for me to revise, do additional research and write the mini-biographies which form the main body of this book. Unfortunately, the College's own records are sometimes sketchy and, furthermore, many of the old boys chose to move elsewhere in the British Empire when they left school. Thereafter the entry gives as much detail about the Old Brightonian's war record and the manner of his death. Where possible, I have drawn on eye-witness accounts and the often very touching letters written, usually by the Commanding Officer, to the grieving families.

A significant difficulty with attempts at commemoration is the need to avoid descending into mawkish sentimentality, or, still worse, the 'tub-thumping jingoism' that Professor Richard Evans feared would characterise the national commemorations of the First World War, as outlined in his article in the *Guardian* of 13 July 2013. The simplest way to avoid such a pitfall, of course, would be not to compile the book at all. But that would be to deny the obvious fact that 149 members of the institution

Opposite: *More Ships, More Food and Earlier Victory.*

Above: *Is Your Home Here? Defend It!*

Top: *Brighton College OTC badges.*

Middle: *Batons used by the Brighton College OTC.*

Above and right: *Two photographs of Brighton College OTC, c. 1914.*

of which myself, my colleagues and my pupils are now a part, died unnaturally in a violent conflict some 100 years ago. On that basis we have a duty, without judging the rights or wrongs of the cause they were fighting for, to give shape and colour to their lives and deaths. Without giving such shape and colour they would simply be a bare list of names on a memorial, names which could, frankly, belong to anyone. It is up to the reader to judge, having read their histories (if such a judgement is possible from what we know) whether their deaths were in vain, in which case they were truly tragic, or whether they did indeed give their lives for a higher purpose, as the former Education Secretary Michael Gove argued in response to Richard Evans.

In addition to the commemorative value, there are some interesting by-products of the research that has gone into this book. While it is obviously not a scientific study, for which it would be necessary to study an entire year group, irrespective of whether they died or even fought in the war, it does provide an interesting insight into the lives and backgrounds of a sample of boys who attended one of Britain's public schools in the late Victorian and Edwardian era. Modern historians are partially responsible for a tendency, much portrayed in such dramas as *Downton Abbey*, to see Britain's pre-1914 society as divided between the cloth-capped masses with little education and not much of a voice, and a limited number of 'toffs', who are portrayed either as benevolent and caring, like Downton's Lord Grantham, or as bellicose and ruthless, like Blackadder's General Melchett. It has been fascinating to observe the lives of the early twentieth century's middle class, which so many modern portrayals of the period ignore, but was in fact the sector of society that both most fervently supported and, arguably, sustained the British war effort. The occupational backgrounds of those who sent their sons to Brighton College before the First World War were particularly revealing. As today, there was a large number of successful professionals – lawyers, architects and engineers in particular (but surprisingly few doctors) – as well as many successful entrepreneurs. The comparison with today cannot be stretched too far: there were many more fathers in the armed forces, and indeed among the clergy, who sent their sons to the college than is the case today. Furthermore, the successful entrepreneurs of the Victorian and Edwardian period had often made their fortune through trade with the Empire, not an avenue open in the early twenty-first century.

A CIVILIAN GUIDE TO THE ARMY.

2ND LIEUTENANT.   LIEUTENANT.   CAPTAIN.

MAJOR.   COLONEL.   GENERAL.

August 12. 1915.

The work has also revealed how globalised the pupils of Brighton College then were; many of the accounts are a vivid demonstration of how the period up to 1914 truly was the first era of globalisation. Many pupils were born in the British Empire, usually in India, and still more emigrated to different parts of the world during their adult lives, something which accounts for the large numbers who were members of the 'dominion contingents'. In this they were more similar to the current pupil body than might be supposed, although they were almost all British subjects; two Frenchmen and one Russian do feature, however. Furthermore, even those who did live in Britain during their childhoods were astonishingly peripatetic, changing addresses regularly, and, in the case of boarders, came from all over the country, not just the South-East. Coupled to this many of them, presumably to the then bursar's dismay, only stayed at the college for one or two years before moving on and comparatively few stayed at the school for a long period, possibly because without national public exams educational continuity was less valued by parents.

In spite of the attempt at objectivity and neutrality given above, I must add that getting to know these Old Boys has been at times an emotional experience. The fabled 'lost generation' is laid out here for close examination, and one cannot help but see in them attributes that are familiar to me among the pupils I teach today. Brilliant all-rounders like Reginald Reeve; sportsmen like Gerald Neame of the Shepherd Neame brewing family; dare-devil risk-takers like Vincent Waterfall, whose passion for speed and technology took him to the earliest death of any British pilot in the war; and the brilliant intellectuals like Keith Scobie, who, like so many of his generation, expressed

Above: *Drawing by Boarding Matron Dorothy Fenwick, 12 August 1915.*

Opposite: *Two images of Brighton College OTC, c. 1914.*

Top: *A current pupil with the statue, June 2016.*

Above: *Brighton College prefects unveil the memorial statue, June 2016.*

himself through poetry. In the development of these and the other 145 pupils had been invested the time and energy of generations of Brighton College staff, whose devastation at the waste of the talent which occurred between the years 1914 and 1918 can only be guessed at. It is, however, the life of Leslie Woodroffe, who, after a glittering academic career which took him from the College to a scholarship at Marlborough and a degree at Oxford, himself became a teacher at Shrewsbury, with which I have been able to empathise the most. Over the past year I have often asked myself whether I would have been capable of 'training' myself 'for sacrifice', in the same way that he, according to one of his Shrewsbury colleagues, did. It is my good fortune that, for all the violence of the early twenty-first-century world, it is a question I will probably, and mercifully, never have to answer, unlike so many of the College's pupils over a century ago.

Max Usher,
Assistant Master,
History Department,
Brighton College,
July 2016

REMEMBERING THE 149
YOUNG MEN FROM
BRIGHTON COLLEGE
WHO GAVE THEIR LIVES IN
THE GREAT WAR 1914-1918

Additional information about the 149 fallen Old Brightonians can be found online at

www.brightoncollegeremembers.com

1914

2nd Lieutenant Vincent Waterfall
(Hampden and Chichester Houses 1907–1909)

Killed in action, Belgium, 22 August 1914 (aged 22)

According to the College Register, Vincent Waterfall was born on 25 May 1892 in Grimsby, Lincolnshire. However, the date of birth given on his aviation certificate was 25 May 1891, a date which is corroborated by the age stated in his entry in the 1901 census. He was the youngest son and tenth child of Walter Waterfall, an engineer, and his wife Mary Anne (née Figgins). During Waterfall's childhood the family moved to Burgess Hill in Sussex where he was educated at Brighton College (Hampden and Chichester) between 1907 and 1909. Little is known about his time at the College save that he was a Corporal in the OTC. However, he was apparently known as 'quite a socialite [who] excelled in many sports and was quite highly regarded'. After leaving the College Waterfall trained at RMC Sandhurst before receiving a commission in the East Yorkshire Regiment on 26 January 1912. He then developed an interest in flying, which led him to transfer to the infant RFC and on 22 April 1913 he obtained his flying certificate. In early 1914 Waterfall won a silver cup in the Brooklands speed-flying competition and was known as a 'dab hand' at flying the extremely flimsy Martin-Handasyde monoplane. A report in the *Surrey Mirror* dated 14 July 1914 records his prosecution for driving a motorcar at the then outrageous speed of 30 mph. The Chairman of the Magistrates warned him that he was 'evidently careless and if you are as careless in your flying it may cost you your life' before fining him £2 plus costs (equivalent to about £200 today).

At the outbreak of war Waterfall was serving with the 5th Squadron Royal Flying Corps, which from 15 August 1914 was based in Maubeuge, France. In the early hours of 22 August 1914, Waterfall flew his first wartime reconnaissance mission, then the sole role of the RFC, which accurately reported that a body of German troops was on the Mons–Soignies Road and turning towards Silly. After returning to base Waterfall and his observer, Lieutenant Charles Bayley, took off again to further observe the progress of the advancing German troops. The events that followed were the subject of a number of eye-witness accounts, but it appears that they flew low over a small

Top: *Vincent Waterfall in his Martin-Handasyde monoplane.*

Above: *Scouts of the Air (airships, aircraft) on a handkerchief.*

group of German troops on the outskirts of the village of Labliau, near Enghien, Belgium. In the words of a German officer on the ground, Captain Walter Bloem:

> Suddenly an airplane flying over us. This time there is no doubt that the red, white and blue rosettes are visible to the naked eye. I order two groups to shoot him, and soon, it seems that everyone is firing. The airplane began a turn, as if he wanted to take a southerly direction, but it's too late: he slumps, made several twists and falls like a stone about a mile from here. Around me, I only hear murmurs of satisfaction. Later three hussars shout us that later they found the plane in a field. I ask them, 'What happened to the pilot and the observer?' 'Both are dead, sir.'

The crash was also observed by a fourteen-year-old Belgian boy, Hector Durand, who had been ordered to deliver grain to the advancing German cavalry. Durand reported that a group of about thirteen German troops after being initially surprised fired shots at a plane that approached them at a very low level and then entered a turn before falling from the sky. After the plane fell from the sky, the smouldering wreckage remained on the ground for some time and as the vast numbers of advancing German troops passed by they removed their hats and saluted. The Germans also took a photograph of the wreckage, among which the bodies of both Waterfall and Bayley are clearly visible.

However, the most detailed account of Waterfall's death and subsequent burial, which presents a contrasting account of how the Germans behaved, was written in rather colourful but slightly broken English by the local Belgian parish priest, Monsignor Kindt, in a letter to Waterfall's sister in 1920 (see overleaf).

In 1924 Waterfall and Bayley were exhumed from their graves in Labliau and reinterred in the Commonwealth War Cemetery in Tournai, Belgium. Commemoration of their deaths has continued until the present day, and on 22 August 2014 a joint Anglo-Belgian memorial was unveiled in Marcq, Belgium, a nearby town, to commemorate the hundredth anniversary of their deaths.

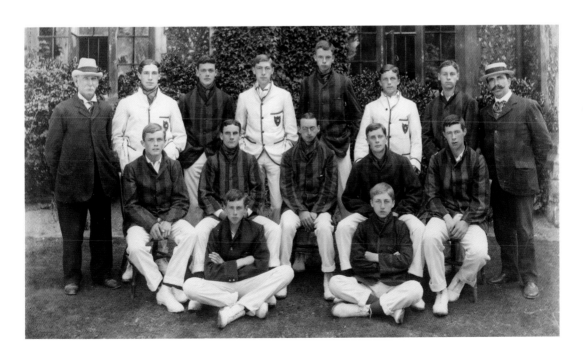

Above: *Vincent Waterfall (back row, third from the left) as part of Brighton College cricket team, 1908.*

Labliau,
near Enghien,
BELGIUM.

9th December, 1920.

Dear Sir,

I received yesterday your letter of inquiries, and at once,
I will give you an answer.

You have been correctly told: Vincent Waterfall, your brave
brother and Bayley, both lieutenants of the English army are
buried, not between Labliau and Enghien, but in the cemetery of
my parish of Labliau, a small village near Enghien (Belgium).
I am parish priest of that little place and nobody better than I
can tell you the truth: from the very beginning I have been the
witness of the all tragedy. On the 22nd of August 1914 when
leaving my church at 9 o'clock in the morning, I saw an English
flying machine turning round my steeple church; I suppose they
were about two hundred yards high, too low for their security.
Indeed, many thousands of German soldiers had left the village
very early in the morning, but a great many of them were still
along the main road, about twenty minutes' walk from the centre
of the place. It was really a great danger for those vaillant
English soldiers who did not know how the matter was. I felt
sorry knowing the greatest danger: with my handkerchief I tried
to show them another direction, and to ascend higher in the sky,
but in vain: perhaps they did not see the signs or did not
understand them. Poor fellows! they went directly to the barbarians. No five minutes after they were fired by platoons, and
I saw the airship raising pendicularly, but being always within
musket-shot, it was frequently touched and came down. I am sure
the brave were killed before reaching the ground.

I never forget that tragedy which occurred in my parish at
the very beginning of the War: it made me ill for a whole week.

Mournful, I ran to the glorious spot, reddened with the
blood of the brave, their eyes closed for ever, amongs wreck,
far from their parents, and own country, surrounded by cruel
foes who like bad dogs were barking terribly, hurrah! hurrah.
God was there to protect their honour, and to cover the sons of
dear old England with the greatest glory. A friend was there
also to represent the family and the native country of those
brave; I was there at once, prepared to do everything necessary:
though I am not English by birth, I am English by heart.

On that occasion I had many troubles and to suffer a great
deal. I was looked on as a spy by those dreadful barbarians,
and several times I had to appear before the "commandantur".
Was I not a friend of English people? I had taught "God save the
King" to Belgian pupils; I had buried by myself in the village
cemetery English soldiers buried in a meadow, etc. etc. All
those miseries are gone and the barbarians also, now I feel happy

(1)

because I have done my duty.

Your dear brother and his fellow Bayley after having been buried coffinless for a fortnight at the very spot where they fell, I took them up and placed each body in a zinc and wooden coffin and took them to our little cemetery.   Each body has a coffin, and here they remain in their resting place.   It will be very consoling for you to know that they are not looked on as strangers.   They are ours, vaillant friends who shed their blood for us and an ideal.   Death has not been dull and gloomy for them, but very glorious!   United in life, in fight and in death, Lieutenants Waterfall and Bayley lay now in the same grave in a poor little village, now faithfull to England's memory.

I take care of the grave by myself.   I dig the earth and plant flowers in the summer.   Allow me to say, the cemetery being behind my garden, very often I pay a Christian visite to their grave and pray for their soul.   Every year on Soul's Day, I go with my people and pray for them.   It is a pity they have got no tombstone, only a poor wooden cross with a French inscription. The cross being too small, I will place another one very soon with the same inscription: Lieutenants Waterfall et Bayley, aviateurs anglais, tués à Labliau le 22 aout 1914.

I have got no photo yet, but I'll care about it very soon, and I'll send you one.

Nothing to pay for that, neither for the past expenses. Though I am poor. I am highly rewarded in getting the opportunity of showing my grateful feelings.   England has shed the blood of her best children for our sake.

My dear sir, excuse my mistakes: I am a poor Belgian father fond of English language, but very imperfectly acquainted with the beauties of Shakespeare's tongue.

This is my address: G. Kindt, curé à Labliau-Mareq, lès Enghien, Belgique.

I won't forget yours.

I remain yours very truly,

(Sgd)   G. KINDT.

Parish Priest.

Captain John Kenneth Tulloch Whish
(School House 1890–1893)

Died of wounds, France, 8 September 1914 (aged 37)

Kenneth Whish was born in Bengal, India on 23 September 1876. He was the only son of Colonel John Tulloch Whish (Indian Army) and his first wife Mary (née Thompson), who were to divorce in 1888. It appears that his father lived abroad almost all his life serving in India and then, after his re-marriage,

Opposite and above: *Letter from G. Kindt, parish priest of Labliau-Mareq Les Enhien, Belgium, to Vincent Waterfall's parents, 9 December 1920.*

moved to France where he died in 1910. His mother appears to have spent more time in Britain and much later to have married a Mr Goodair and settled in Kent. After his parents divorced and his mother had moved back to Britain, Whish was a pupil at the College, after which he became a cadet at RMC Sandhurst. Whish received a commission in the Essex Regiment on 29 April 1895 and later transferred to the East Surrey Regiment and accompanied its 2nd Battalion to the Boer War in 1899. After the conclusion of the Boer War he continued to serve with the East Surrey Regiment and by the outbreak of war in 1914 had been promoted to Captain.

In August 1914 the 1st Battalion, East Surrey Regiment, formed part of 5th Division. Whish joined his battalion on 7 September 1914 while it was involved as reinforcements in the Battle of the Marne. He was killed in action the next day, 8 September 1914, possibly by friendly shellfire, during a series of skirmishes that took place as the German Army retreated after encountering the BEF.

Whish is buried in the Perreuse Chateau Franco-British Cemetery, Seine-et-Marne, France.

Lieutenant Geoffrey Stewart Augustus White (Hampden House 1901–1903)

Killed in action, Belgium, 10 September 1914 (aged 23)

Geoffrey White was born in Wandsworth, London on 18 August 1891. He was the middle son of Colonel George Augustus White, sometime commanding officer 1st Battalion, South Lancashire Regiment, and his second wife Alice (*née* Slater). Shortly after White's birth the family moved to Hove and White attended the College for two years during which time he won the Glenday Cup for athletics and a Latin Prize. In 1903 the family moved again, to Godalming, Surrey, and it is unknown where White completed his education.

White trained as a cadet at RMC Sandhurst and in March 1910 received a commission in the South Lancashire Regiment. He was attached to the 2nd Battalion, South Lancashires, which formed part of 3rd Division, with which he landed in France on 14 August 1914 and fought at the Battle

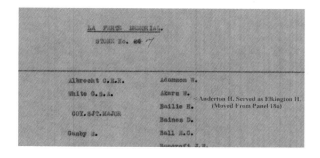

Top: *Captain John Kenneth Tulloch Whish, 1st Battalion, East Surrey Regiment.*

Above left: *Lieutenant Geoffrey Stewart Augustus White (BCRH).*

Above right: *Panel list made by the Commonwealth War Graves Commission, which includes an entry for Lieutenant Geoffrey Stewart Augustus White.*

of Mons. He was reported missing on 26 August 1914 during the subsequent retreat and his death was listed as 'accepted' on 10 September 1914.

White has no known grave but is commemorated on the La Ferté-sous-Jouarre Memorial, France.

2nd Lieutenant Neil James Robert Wright (School House 1908–1911)

Killed in action, France, 15 September 1914 (aged 20)

Neil Wright was born on 4 February 1894 in Teddington, Middlesex. He was the second child and only son of James Wright, an agent, and his wife Leticia (*née* Brown). The family then moved to Sevenoaks, Kent and, after James Wright's death, to Essex. After Wright was a pupil at the College he became a cadet at RMA Woolwich before receiving a commission in the Royal Field Artillery in August 1913.

Wright was attached to the 15th Brigade RFA, which formed part of 5th Division. He disembarked with the brigade at Boulogne, France, on 19 August 1914 and subsequently took part in the retreat from Mons and the Battle of the Marne. He was killed in action on 15 September 1914 while involved in the pursuit to the Aisne following the German defeat in the Battle of the Marne.

Wright's grave is in Vendresse British Cemetery, Aisne, France.

Above: *Artillery Wood Cemetery, Ypres, Belgium.*

Below: *School House, 1908, when Neil Wright attended.*

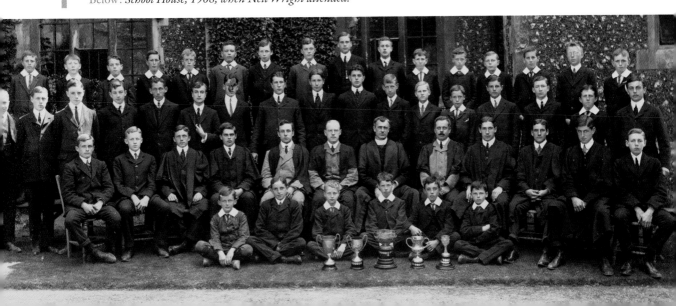

Private Louis Paul Veyrier-Montagnères (Durnford House 1909–1910)

Killed in action, France, 18 September 1914 (aged 23)

Louis Paul Veyrier-Montagnères, known to the College as Paul, was born in Bordeaux, France on 20 January 1891. He was the second son and third child of James Veyrier-Montagnères, Mayor of Arcachon, France from 1897 to 1922, and his wife Mathilde (*née* Mateo-Petit), a nurse. It is unclear why Veyrier-Montagnères spent a year boarding at the College but it was probably to learn English as the last stage of his education.

In 1911, after leaving the College, he was conscripted into the French Army and served in the 18e Régiment d'Infanterie, which formed part of the French 36th Division. On the outbreak of war in 1914 he was still serving in the army because of the three-year law passed in 1913, which extended the term of conscription in France from two to three years in response to the declining birth rate. He was killed in action on the Aisne on 18 September 1914 during the advance that followed the Battle of the Marne.

Unfortunately, it has not been possible to ascertain where Veyrier-Montagnères is buried due to the lack of a central French War Graves register. He is, however, listed and commemorated in the register of war dead published by the French Ministry of Defence.

Above: *Hargrave Curtis (back row first left) as part of Brighton College football team, 1901–02.*

Captain Hargrave Tindal Raleigh Curtis
(Hampden 1899–1902)

Died of illness, India, 27 September 1914 (aged 29)

Hargrave Curtis was born on 28 September 1884 in Brighton. He was the only son of Reverend Francis Curtis and his wife Jane to survive to adulthood. Curtis's parents married in India but had moved to Brighton by the time Curtis was born and lived there while he was a pupil at the College. On leaving school Curtis went to RMC Sandhurst and received a commission in the Royal Berkshire Regiment in 1904 and a further two promotions to Captain by 1914.

On the outbreak of war Curtis was attached to the 2nd Battalion, Royal Berkshire Regiment in India. However, on 27 September 1914 he died there of an unknown disease before the battalion was sent to Europe along with the other regular battalions stationed around the British Empire.

Curtis's grave is in Deolali Government Cemetery, Bombay, India.

Private Rodolphe Emile Armbruster
(School House 1911–1912)

Killed in action, France, 23 October 1914 (aged 21)

Rodolphe Emile Armbruster was born on 10 August 1893 in the 9e Arrondissement of Paris, France. His father was Emile Armbruster, an hotelier who was to become the Managing Director of the Hotel Plaza Athénée in Paris, and his wife Julie. It is not known whether he had any siblings. There are few records of Armbruster in the College archive but it is probable that he spent a year at school in England aged 18 in order to complete his education by learning English. If he intended to follow his father into the Paris hotel business then fluent English would presumably have been a useful skill. After he left Brighton College it seems likely that he was conscripted straight into the French Army to do compulsory military service as all young Frenchmen were obliged to do (and following the three year law[1]). At the outbreak of war he was already a serving soldier.

His regiment was the 13e Régiment d'Infanterie, which formed part of the French 16th Division, and he started the war on the Alsace-Lorraine Front, much further south than the BEF's theatre of operations.

On 23 October 1914 Armbruster was killed in action with his regiment while it was involved in heavy fighting at Apremont-la-Forêt on the River Meuse. The forest was set ablaze by enemy action and it was in this context that Armbruster lost his life but it is unknown whether he was killed by the blaze or by enemy fire.

Armbruster's grave is in the Nécropole nationale Vaux-Racine, Saint-Mihiel, Meuse, France.

Above: *Private Rodolphe Emile Armbruster (BCRH).*

1 *For further information see the entry for Paul Veyrier-Montagnères.*

Colonel Charles Arthur Cecil King
(Mr Allum's 1877–1881)

Killed in action, Belgium, 30 October 1914 (aged 51)

Colonel King was born in 1863 in Cape Town, Cape Colony (now South Africa). He was the second son and fifth child of James King, a merchant, and his wife Rebecca (*née* Little). King married Adela Margaret Eley in 1895, but the couple had no children. After attending the College, King trained as an army officer and received a commission in the Yorkshire Regiment. In 1885 he saw service on the Nile expedition, which attempted to relieve the ill-fated Gordon at Khartoum, during which he fought at the battle of Ginnis, being awarded the Khedive's Star the following year. In 1892 he was involved in an operation in the Katchin Hills, Burma, after which he was promoted to Captain. In 1900, following the start of the First Boer War, he was appointed Adjutant in the 3rd Battalion, Yorkshire Regiment and was mentioned in despatches for his coolness and effectiveness in action. After the conclusion of the Boer War he was promoted relatively swiftly, reaching in the rank of Colonel in December 1913.

On the outbreak of war King was given command of the 2nd Battalion Yorkshire Regiment, also known as the Green Howards, which formed part of 7th Division – the first division to be despatched to France that was not part of the original BEF. He landed with the battalion in Belgium on 6 October 1914 and played a crucial role in the First Battle of Ypres. From 16 October until 27 October the battalion held the crossroads at Gheluvelt and suffered very heavy casualties before being withdrawn to rest at Sanctuary Wood. Unfortunately, however, the period of rest was curtailed because increasing German pressure meant that the BEF, still a very small force compared with the mass army it was to become, had to throw in its last reserves. The battalion went into line again the next day and King was killed in action on 30 October 1914. The account given in the regimental history states the following:

> At last on the 27th, we were moved back to SANCTUARY WOOD for a rest, but no sooner had we bivouacked, than the order came to move up into the advanced fire trenches immediately. The exhausted

men, comfortably fixed up for the night, kits, blankets, camp kettles, etc. brought up from YPRES, fell in at once and no one grumbled. The Colonel was very ill and worn out, but nothing would keep him from his men.

On the morning of the 29th, the enemy succeeded in breaking through a Regiment on our left, and threatened our left rear. The Line was forced to fall back under devastating fire for about half a mile – two platoons of 'A' Company being the last to retire. Colonel King then reorganized the battalion, collected anyone he could lay hands on from other Units, formed them up in the road, and led an attack with this scratch force. Colonel King's prompt and gallant action and the magnificent way it was carried out once again 'saved the Line.' Next day in an attack of overwhelming numbers of infantry and appalling bombardment, Colonel King was killed among very heavy losses of officers and men. Still the men held on, and no enemy passed the GREEN HOWARDS, nor did the battalion give a yard. Their strength was now three hundred, a Captain in command.

Following his death one of his fellow officers wrote:

The bald statement of [Charles King's] distinguished services … in no way conveys the sense of personal bereavement which is felt by those of all ranks who had the privilege of serving with him. The cheeriest, kindliest and most generous of friends. He was beloved by both his brother officers and by the men who served under him, taking a keen interest in all sports; he encouraged and shared in all their amusements. How many a dull hour did he brighten for his comrades. How many a dreary station became happier and livelier for his presence! No kinder or more genial host could be found; his hospitality was proverbial and he was never happier than when entertaining his friends. The thrilling story of those last few eventful days before his death is a story that will live long in the annals of our Army, telling of a heroic struggle against well-nigh overwhelming odds. In this struggle he played a splendid part.

King has no known grave but is commemorated on the Menin Gate, Ypres, Belgium.

Private Harley Norman Duff (School House 1912–1913)

Killed in action, Belgium, 1 November 1914 (aged 18)

Harley Duff was born on 9 June 1896 in Wandsworth, London. He was the only son and eldest child of Norman Duff, an accountant, and his wife Alice (née Homan). By 1912, when Duff was briefly a pupil at the College, the family was living in Purley, Surrey.

Opposite: *Colonel Charles Arthur Cecil King MID. Unit: 2nd Battalion, Yorkshire.*

Above: *Officers of the Second Battalion the Yorkshire Regiment, October 1914. Colonel Charles King is the older officer seated fifth from the left in the second row, behind the dog.*

On the outbreak of war in summer 1914 he was enrolled in the 14th Battalion, London Regiment (London Scottish) – a territorial unit, which unlike most territorial units was sent to France relatively quickly in the autumn of 1914. The battalion landed in France in mid-October 1914 and was attached to the BEF Cavalry Corps, which had a small infantry component in addition to its horsed formations. The battalion was engaged in heavy fighting in the Messines area from 30 October onwards and Duff was killed in action on 1 November 1914 after having served for only three months.

Duff has no known grave but is commemorated on the Menin Gate, Ypres, Belgium. The discrepancy in place between Messines, where he was apparently killed, and Ypres, where he was commemorated, is probably accounted for by the fact that from 7 November the London Scottish formed part of 1st Division, which fought at Ypres.

2nd Lieutenant Ernest Lionel Lane-Anderson (Durnford 1909–1910)

Killed in action, Belgium, 10 November 1914 (aged 20)

Ernest Lane-Anderson was born on 24 December 1893 in Calcutta, India. He was the son of George Lane-Anderson, who was 'of private means', by his first wife, whose name remains unknown. In 1899 Lane-Anderson's father married again to Monica (*née* Dear) and had two further children. By 1909 the family had moved to Britain from India and lived in Hove. While Lane-Anderson was briefly a pupil at the College he was in the 2nd XI football and cricket teams. After leaving the College he studied for his army exams

Top: *Men of the London Gunners Regiment in a rural billet, in the Abbots Langley area, August/September 1914.*

Left: *2nd Lieutenant Ernest Lionel Lane-Anderson (BCRH).*

and in 1912 enrolled at RMC Sandhurst. Following graduation from Sandhurst in 1913 he received a commission in the Royal Scots Fusiliers.

On the outbreak of war he was attached to the 1st Battalion Royal Scots Fusiliers, which formed part of 3rd Division BEF and landed in France on 14 August 1914 as part of the original BEF. He was mentioned in despatches by Sir John French (Commander-in-Chief of the BEF) on 8 October 1914 following his conduct in the advance following the Battle of the Marne. The 1st Battalion Scots Fusiliers was involved in heavy fighting during the First Battle of Ypres and it was there that Lane-Anderson was killed in action on 10 November 1914, probably in the Bixschoote area.

Lane-Anderson has no known grave but is commemorated on the Menin Gate, Ypres, Belgium.

Lieutenant Lionel Gaisford (School House 1902–1905)

Died of wounds, France, 23 November 1914 (aged 26)

Lionel Gaisford was born on 12 June 1888 in Quetta, India. He was the eldest child of Lieutenant Colonel Gilbert Gaisford, Indian Army, and his wife Laura (*née* Hutchinson). In 1898 Gaisford's father was murdered while acting as a 'Political Agent' in Balochistan, India and the family then returned to Britain where they lived in Ealing, London, until his mother died on board a ship off the French coast in 1905. During the period up to his mother's death Gaisford was educated in Britain, first in a prep school in the Wirral and then at Brighton College. After leaving the College Gaisford became a cadet at RMC Sandhurst and received a commission in the Royal Irish Rifles before transferring to the 58th Vaughan's Rifles, an Indian Army regiment, in 1907. He saw active service in 1908 with the Mohmand Expedition on India's North-West Frontier.

On the outbreak of war in 1914 the regiment formed part of 7th Meerut Division, which was sent to the Western Front as part of the Indian Expeditionary Force operating in support of the BEF. The force disembarked at Marseilles on 30 September 1914 and was rapidly sent into action against the Germans in the campaign that culminated in the First Battle of Ypres. On 23 November 1914 Gaisford was involved in an attack on German trenches in the La Bassée District and sustained wounds from which he died the following day.

Gaisford's grave is in Béthune Town Cemetery, France.

Above: *Lieutenant Lionel Gaisford, 58th Vaughan's Rifles, Frontier Force, Indian Army.*

Right: *Brighton College football team, 1904. Gaisford stands in the back row with arms folded.*

1915

Troops landing on C Beach, Suvla Bay, late on 7 August 1915.

Lieutenant Reginald Thomas Buckingham Pope (Junior House 1901–1904)

Killed in action, Belgium, 16 February 1915 (aged 23)

Reginald was born in Brighton on 29 July 1891. He was the eldest son and second child, of six, of Reginald Barrett Pope, a solicitor, and his wife Mary (*née* Reid). While living in Brighton he was a member of Junior House between 1901 and 1904 before proceeding first to Rottingdean School and then to Bradfield College, where he was a keen cricketer. After Bradfield he went to RMC Sandhurst in 1911 where he graduated twenty-third in his cohort of cadets and subsequently received a commission as 2nd Lieutenant in the 1st Battalion Welsh Regiment on 23 September 1911. From then until the outbreak of war Pope served with the Welsh Regiment in Egypt, the Sudan and India, being promoted to Lieutenant on 16 July 1912. Regimental records indicate that while in the Sudan he enjoyed shooting big game with his fellow officers around the source of the White Nile.

On the outbreak of war, because it was then stationed in India, the 1st Battalion Welsh Regiment, which formed part of 28th Division, was one of the last of the original regular battalions to arrive on the Western Front, arriving in January 1915. On 16 February 1915 the battalion was in line near Ypres when it was subjected to a flank attack by the enemy which, although not part of a major offensive, inflicted heavy losses, including Pope, who was killed in action. Following his death Pope's commanding officer wrote to his brother:

> We had a most terrible time ... Your brother thought he had seen a sniper and got up with a rifle to try and shoot him, when almost immediately he was hit right through

the forehead. He died at once without any suffering at all. When night fell I managed to get his body back and had him sent out of the trenches. He is buried at Chateau Rosenthal, Ypres between Capt. Lloyd and another officer.

Pope's grave is now in the Bedford House Cemetery, near Ypres, Belgium. He is also commemorated in a stained glass window depicting St Oswald, gifted by his mother to St Mary's Church, Kemptown, Brighton. St Oswald was a Christian warrior king of Northumbria killed while fighting the pagan Mercians in 641. The Pope family name lives on in the Burgess Hill solicitors' firm Stevens Son and Pope.

Top: *Allied and Central Powers map on a handkerchief.*

Opposite left: *Lieutenant Reginald Thomas Buckingham Pope (BCRH).*

Opposite right: *The image of St Oswald was created in memory of Reginald Pope as one of the memorial windows in St Mary's Church, Brighton.*

2nd Lieutenant William Hugh Coxon (Chichester House 1907–1911)

Killed in action, France, 11 March 1915 (aged 21)

William Hugh Coxon was born on 19 August 1893 in Derby. He was the youngest son and fourth child of Thomas Coxon, a solicitor, and his wife Edith (*née* Cox). Coxon entered the College in 1907 thanks to a Maths scholarship funded by a firm called Bouch and Pochin. While at the College he was an active debater, and is recorded as speaking in favour of Home Rule for Ireland in one very contentious debate. It is unclear what his occupation was between leaving school in 1911 and the outbreak of war in 1914. In September 1914 he volunteered for the Nottinghamshire and Derby Regiment (the Sherwood Foresters) and received a commission as a 2nd Lieutenant in the 1st Battalion, Sherwood Foresters in January 1915.

He was killed in action with D Company, 1st Battalion, Sherwood Foresters at 4pm on 11 March 1915 at the Battle of Neuve Chapelle (10–13 March, 1915). The company made four unsuccessful attempts to take a German machine gun position, which involved charging across a 100–200 yard stretch of No Man's Land; one account of the action describes them as being 'shot down like targets at a fairground'. He was among nine officers in the 1st Sherwood Foresters who were killed out of eighteen present at the start of the action.

Coxon is commemorated on Le Touret Memorial, France.

Captain Henry Etlinger (Junior House 1890–1893)

Died of wounds, Belgium, 27 April 1915 (aged 35)

Henry Etlinger was born in 1880, probably in India, then part of the British Empire. His father was George E. Etlinger, a retired Indian Army officer who later settled in St John's Wood, London, but his mother's identity is unknown to us because she did not later return to Britain. While he was a pupil at the College the family was still living abroad and there are no remaining records of either his senior school or his occupation between leaving school and the start of the First World War. However, his rank in 1914 suggests that he was a professional soldier and it is certainly possible that having left senior school, he received a commission in the Indian Army shortly afterwards and then served there until 1914.

Top: *2nd Lieutenant William Hugh Coxon (BCRH).*

Left: *Henry Etlinger a member of Brighton College choir, 1892.*

In 1914 Etlinger was a Captain in the 19th Bhopal Infantry Regiment of the Indian Army, which was attached to Meerut Division. The Meerut Division, along with one other infantry division and a division of Indian cavalry, formed the Indian Corps, which landed in Southern France in autumn 1914 to form part of the BEF. It was while serving on the Western Front, during the Second Battle of Ypres, that Henry Etlinger was wounded; he died of his wounds the same day, on 27 April 1915.

Etlinger has no known grave but is commemorated on the Menin Gate, Ypres, Belgium.

Private Edward Clinton Baddeley
(School House 1889–1893)

Killed in action, Belgium, 8 May 1915 (aged 38)

Edward Baddeley was born in Madras, India, on 2 July 1876. He was the second son of Colonel William Baddeley OB and his wife Catherine (*née* Daniell). Details about his time at the College are scarce, although it appears that for a brief period his mother may have resided in Brighton and then elsewhere in Britain while her son was a pupil at the College. However, she certainly then returned to India where she died in 1897. Baddeley did not join the army immediately after leaving school but in 1900 received a commission in the Imperial Regular Forces. He served in the West India Regiment and later received a commission in the Railway Pioneers, from which he was discharged in September 1902, following the end of the Boer War. An announcement was posted in the *London Gazette* stating: 'Edward C Baddeley is removed from the Army, His Majesty having no further occasion for his services.' This might suggest that his departure from the army was because of some form of poor behaviour but no further records about an Edward C. Baddeley could be found in the UK. However, at some point between 1902 and 1914 someone with exactly the same name settled in Western Canada and it is the death of this Baddeley that appears to be recorded on the Roll of Honour compiled by the College in the 1920s.

Top: *Officers of the 2nd Battalion The Prince of Wales (North Staffordshire Regiment) outside the officers' mess in Multan, India, 1908. Henry Etlinger is standing fourth from the left, in the back row.*

Shortly after the outbreak of war in 1914, the 'Canadian' Baddeley apparently enlisted as a private in the 30th Battalion Canadian Regiment. In March 1915 he was sent as a replacement draft to France and then fought in the dying stages of the Second Battle of Ypres with Princess Patricia's Canadian Light Infantry. On 8 May 1915 he was reported missing following fighting in the Bellewaerde Lake area. Intriguingly he listed his next of kin as a Mrs E.R. Hughes of Montgomery Apartments, Portland, Oregon, USA, then a neutral country.

Baddeley has no known grave but is commemorated on the Menin Gate, Ypres, Belgium. The elder brother of the 'British' Baddeley, Charles, was killed in the Boer War.

Lieutenant Leonard Nithsdale Walford (Hampden House 1909–1911)

Killed in action, Belgium, 8 May 1915 (aged 19)

Leonard Walford was born on 10 December 1896 in Middlesex. He was the only son of Edward Walford, a stockbroker, and his wife Laura Walford. Although originally from the London area, the family had moved to Brighton by 1901. While Walford was at the College he was described by one master as 'stubborn but [with] great potential' and was an enthusiastic member of the OTC. After leaving the College Walford enrolled as a Law undergraduate at London University and the Middle Temple in 1913 and shortly thereafter he joined the Inns of Court Officer Training Corps.

At the outbreak of war in August 1914 Walford received a commission in the 12th Battalion London Regiment, owing to his prior officer training with the highly regarded Inns of Court OTC. He was subsequently promoted to Lieutenant in September 1914. It was in this unit that he was to be killed in action on 8 May 1915 during the last days of the Second Battle of Ypres. The 12th Battalion, London Regiment, which now formed part of 28th Division, was called forward to reinforce the line and Walford volunteered to go 100 yards in front of the main body in order to reconnoitre the crest of a ridge. While on the crest he came under heavy artillery fire and after a high explosive shell burst within 6 feet of him he was never seen again.

Walford has no known grave but his death is commemorated on the Menin Gate, Ypres, Belgium. A contributor to the *Bonds of Sacrifice*, a record of lawyers killed in the Great War, wrote that he had 'a very high opinion of him [Walford], he was a good boy and full of intelligence … his calling was as a lawyer, he has died a brutal death and I am proud of him.'

Above: *Lieutenant Leonard Nithsdale Walford. Unit: 1st/12th (County of London) Battalion, London Regiment (The Rangers).*

Lance-Corporal Val Oram Penruddock Lander (Hampden 1909–1912)

Killed in action, France, 9 May 1915 (aged 21)

Val Lander was born in Hammersmith, London, on 14 February 1894. He was the eldest son of six children of Charles Oram Lander, an American actor who lived and worked in London, and his wife Emily (née Clarke). He had two brothers and four sisters. By 1911, while Lander was at the College, the family had moved to 2 Powis Square, Notting Hill. After he left the College Lander's immediate movements or occupation are not known but it appears clear that he was resident in London and described himself as a 'student for Mercantile Service'.

In August 1914 Lander enlisted at the Kensington recruiting station into the 13th (Princess Louise's Kensington) Battalion, London Regiment and was promoted to Lance-Corporal in the ensuing expansion of the army over the winter of 1914/15. The 13th Battalion landed at Le Havre on 4 November 1914 and was then attached to 8th Division. Lander was killed in action on 9 May 1915 while taking part in the attack on Auber's Ridge, which was conceived as a diversionary operation to coincide with the much bigger French attack in Artois, which began on the same day. Lander was also, unusually for an NCO, mentioned in despatches following the action.

Lander's body was never found but he is commemorated on the Ploegsteert Memorial, Ypres, Belgium. In addition, a number of items, including confirmation of his posthumous mention in despatches, his service medals and an army button, which his family converted into a remembrance brooch, have been deposited in the National Archives with his Service Record.

Top: *Lance Corporal Val Oram Lander, 1/13th (County of London) Princess Louise's Kensington Battalion, The London Regiment, 1914.*

Above: *Star medal and button belonging to Lance Corporal Val Oram Lander.*

Lieutenant Isaac Althorp Ridgway
(School House 1901–1904)

Died of wounds, Turkey, 12 May 1915 (aged 28)

Isaac Ridgway was born on 24 August 1886 in Lymm, Cheshire. He was the youngest son and fourth child of Thomas Ridgway, a solicitor, and his wife Emily (*née* Dawbarn). After the College he went to Victoria University, Manchester, now part of Manchester University, from which he graduated with both a BSc and, in 1910, a Masters degree in Engineering. In 1911 he became a member of the Institute of Civil Engineers. He then emigrated to Australia, becoming in July 1911 the Chief Engineer at Freemantle Dock, Queensland, and in December 1913 responsible for all the lighthouses on the Queensland coast. Owing to the importance of his job he had great difficulty obtaining permission to leave the lighthouse service to volunteer for the Australian Imperial Force, the Australian component of the famous ANZACs, on the outbreak of war. However, on 16 December 1914 he received his commission as a 2nd Lieutenant in the 6th Battalion, Australian Imperial Force, which formed part of 1st Australian Division.

With the rest of the ANZACs Ridgway sailed to Egypt and then participated in the landings at Gallipoli on 25 April 1915. On 8 May 1915, during the advance on Krithia, he was hit by two bullets, which caused severe wounds to his epigastrium, upper torso, and bladder, from which he died on 12 May 1915 aboard the hospital ship HMHS *Braemar Castle*.

Ridgway was buried at sea but is commemorated on the Lone Pine Memorial at Gallipoli, Turkey. He is also commemorated on a carved angel in St John's Church, Freemantle, Australia. In March 1916 a letter from Ridgway's parents was received by the Department of Trade and Customs in Melbourne, Australia, enquiring about his personal effects. It is unknown whether they had a satisfactory response but it seems unlikely, because in 2008 a kit bag containing the personal belongings of 'Lt I.A. Ridgway 6th Battalion, AIF', was found during a house clearance in Canberra.

Captain Gordon Belcher
(Junior and School Houses 1894–1904)

Killed in action, Belgium, 16 May 1915 (aged 29)

Gordon Belcher was born in Kemptown, Brighton on 26 September 1885. He was one of four sons of Reverend Thomas Belcher, Head Master of the school between 1881 and 1893. After attending the College, where he was a prominent member of the 1st XI cricket team, he went up to St Catharine's College, Cambridge, from where he graduated in 1907. While at Cambridge he played first-class cricket for Hampshire before representing Berkshire in the minor counties' championship between 1910 and 1913.

A UNIQUE PICTURE OF THE 1st BERKS AT THE FRONT.

A 1st Berks fortified house in trench. Reading from left to right: Corporal Jarvis, Private Burls, wounded; Captain Gordon Belcher (Berks County Cricketer), killed; Corporal Nelhams, wounded; Private Bridgeman, missing.

Opposite: *School House, 1903, when Isaac Ridgway was in attendance.*

Above left: *Gordon Belcher in the Brighton College cricket team, 1903.*

Above right: *A group from the 1st Battalion, Berkshire Regt depicted in a dugout, originally published in a local newspaper. Gordon Belcher is seated in the centre of the picture.*

Shortly after the outbreak of war he received a commission in the Royal Berkshire Regiment and was attached to the 1st Battalion, which formed part of 2nd Division. He was awarded the MC on 18 February 1915 (although the actual document of citation does not appear to have survived) after which he continued to serve and was killed in action near Richebourg L'Avoué, Belgium, on May 16 1915 during the last stages of the Second Battle of Ypres.

Belcher is buried in the Commonwealth War Cemetery at Rue-des-Berceaux, Richebourg-L'Avoué, France. A stained-glass window in the chapel in the school commemorates the lives and sacrifice of Belcher and his two brothers, Raymond Belcher OB and Harold Belcher OB. His paternal first cousin Basil Belcher OB and his maternal first cousins Gerald Tassel-Neame OB and Geoffrey Neame OB were all also killed in the war. His other brother, Arthur Belcher OB, was Head Master of the College between 1933 and 1937.

Captain Albert Arundel Holmes (School House 1885–1888)

Died of pneumonia, Great Britain, 19 May 1915 (aged 43)

Albert Holmes was born in Upminster on 9 November 1871. He was the second son and fifth child of Lieutenant-Colonel Henry Holmes, an army officer turned brewer, and his wife Emilie (née Wagener). He had four brothers, one of whom later settled in South Africa, and one sister. While the family continued to live in Essex, where Henry Holmes was the proprietor of Hornchurch Brewery, Albert Holmes was sent to the College in 1885. After leaving the College he appears to have received a part-time commission in the Volunteer Artillery (a forerunner of the Territorial Army) while pursuing a career in insurance, becoming a successful Lloyds underwriter while also pursuing a career as a farmer.

Top: *Gordon Belcher's obituary in Wisden, 1916.*

Left: *Captain Albert Arundel Holmes (BCRH).*

He married Ellen (*née* Lambard) at St Barnabas Church, Mayland, Essex, and subsequently fathered four children, later moving to Northiam, Sussex.

Following the outbreak of war in 1914, Holmes was rapidly re-commissioned as a Captain and training officer in the Royal Sussex Regiment despite his artillery background and relatively advanced age. It was in the course of training this battalion that in March 1915 he contracted the illness that was eventually to kill him. The circumstances of his death were set out in great detail by the Medical Officer of the battalion, Captain Mansell, in a letter he sent to the Regiment's Headquarters, now preserved in Lloyds' First World War Records. The letter not only details the circumstances of his death but also provides an interesting insight into the character of the man and the fact that he was probably not fit enough for the military duties he had been asked to undertake:

> Captain Holmes was a keen and enthusiastic soldier and very devoted to his work. By no means a strong man, he was very active and wiry. There was a heart bruit to be heard over the aortic region, but this had not been a barrier to his taking part in shooting and lawn tennis, both of which sports he was very fond of …
>
> He was known to complain of some fatigue after route marching. The deceased had been in good health up to 28 March 1915, on which date he took his Company over to Northiam for some field training. He remained there up to the 4th of April when the Company returned to Hastings … weather during that time was excessively cold and wet and the men suffered accordingly. From April 4th deceased suffered from a cold and on April 22nd developed influenza and was in a low and depressed state of mind. On April 25th pneumonia set in and developed very rapidly into a very severe attack …
>
> During the next week delirium of a very marked kind set in, his servant being required as well as the nurses in attendance to restrain his movements. The delirium took the form of raving about his military duties and at times he would start up in bed and give military orders to his servant as if on parade. Apart from this delirium, the pneumonia gradually subsided under treatment, and, on May 8 the patient was so far well that it was proposed to remove him to his home at Northiam during the following week. The next day, in the early morning, an acute abdominal attack occurred, giving rise to great pain in the epigastric and hepatic regions, accompanied by vomiting and marked rigors. A condition of general peritonitis developed, and the patient died on the May 19th …
>
> I am of the opinion that the death of the late Captain A.A. Holmes was directly attributable to the stress of military service and to the fact that he suffered from wet and exposure while training his company at Northiam.

Holmes's grave is in St Andrews Churchyard, Hornchurch, Essex, where many of his siblings still lived. He is also commemorated on the memorial at Lloyds of London.

Lieutenant John Cecil Stollery (Hampden House 1901–1902)

Killed in action, Belgium, 24 May 1915 (aged 28)

John Stollery was born on 27 August 1886 in London. He was the only son and second child of John Stollery, a clothes manufacturer, and his wife Helen (*née* Bulleid). In 1900 the family moved to Hove and Stollery spent a year at the College before completing his education at

Right: *Lieutenant John Cecil Stollery (BCRH).*

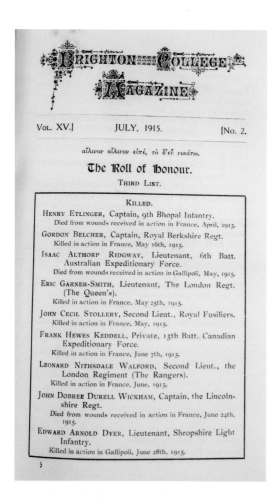

BRIGHTON COLLEGE MAGAZINE

Vol. XV.]   JULY, 1915.   [No. 2.

αἴλινον αἴλινον εἰπέ, τὸ δ'εὖ νικάτω.

The Roll of Honour.

THIRD LIST.

KILLED.

HENRY ETLINGER, Captain, 9th Bhopal Infantry.
Died from wounds received in action in France, April, 1915.

GORDON BELCHER, Captain, Royal Berkshire Regt.
Killed in France, May 16th, 1915.

ISAAC ALTHORP RIDGWAY, Lieutenant, 6th Batt. Australian Expeditionary Force.
Died from wounds received in action in Gallipoli, May, 1915.

ERIC GARNER-SMITH, Lieutenant, The London Regt. (The Queen's).
Killed in action in France, May 25th, 1915.

JOHN CECIL STOLLERY, Second Lieut., Royal Fusiliers.
Killed in action in France, May, 1915.

FRANK HEWES KEDDELL, Private, 15th Batt. Canadian Expeditionary Force.
Killed in action in France, June 7th, 1915.

LEONARD NITHSDALE WALFORD, Second Lieut., the London Regiment (The Rangers).
Killed in action in France, June, 1915.

JOHN DOBREE DURELL WICKHAM, Captain, the Lincolnshire Regt.
Died from wounds received in action in France, June 24th, 1915.

EDWARD ARNOLD DYER, Lieutenant, Shropshire Light Infantry.
Killed in action in Gallipoli, June 28th, 1915.

5

Cottesmore School, Hove. In 1907 he went up to Christ Church, Oxford, to read Law, joining the Oxford University Rifle Volunteer Corps in 1909 and graduating in 1910. He was called to the Bar in 1911, started practising as a barrister in London and joined the Inns of Court OTC in 1913.

On the outbreak of war he applied for and received a commission in the Royal Fusiliers, stating in his application that he had 'a good working knowledge of French and German'. However, on 22 August 1914 he was despatched to France with the 1st Battalion, Warwickshire Regiment, a regular unit which formed part of the original BEF. It was unusual for someone who volunteered on the outbreak of war to be sent to the front so quickly but it may have been because of his linguistic abilities. After seeing action at Le Cateau and on the Marne, Stollery was invalided home on 17 November 1914 because he was suffering from neurasthenia, what has become known to posterity as 'shell-shock'. On 17 December the proceedings of a medical board stated he was 'suffering from nervous breakdown and sleeplessness due to shell fire in the trenches' but he was nonetheless passed fit to return to the front and received a full commission in the 3rd Battalion, Royal Fusiliers on 23 December 1914. He returned to France five days later and was promoted to Lieutenant on 23 February 1915. On 24 May 1915 the 3rd Battalion were to the south of the Ypres–Roulers railway line when the Germans launched a gas attack. By the end of the day they had suffered sixteen officer casualties. One of these was Stollery, who, in the words of the subsequent death announcement in *The Times*, was killed by a sniper 'whilst uttering words of encouragement to his men'.

Stollery has no known grave but is commemorated on the Menin Gate, Ypres, Belgium.

Lieutenant Eric John Garner-Smith (Hampden House 1907–1908)

Killed in action, France, 25 May 1915 (aged 23)

Eric Garner-Smith was born on 17 March 1892 in Sydenham, London. He was the eldest son of John Garner-Smith, an insurance broker, and his wife Louise Abbey Hutton. Garner-Smith's only sibling, his brother Gerard, also attended the College. The family were itinerant, moving from

Above: *The Roll of Honour published in the* Brightonian Magazine, *December 1916, showing John Stollery's entry.*

Sydenham to Bristol, then to Penge in 1901 and presumably to the Brighton area when the Garner-Smith brothers were dayboys at the College, before emigrating to New York in May 1911. Garner-Smith was an 'articled clerk' after leaving school, presumably for either a firm of solicitors or accountants. Although he spent some time in America it is clear that either on or before the outbreak of war in 1914 he had returned to Britain. He then received a commission as a 2nd Lieutenant in the 24th Battalion, London Regiment in September 1914.

The battalion was sent to France in March 1915 as part of the 142nd Brigade. Of his first experience in action Garner-Smith wrote:

> I had a beastly half hour before starting … drumming into my head over and over again that I must not let the men think I was at all funky … as soon as we got off I was all right, and only once in the four days we were in line was I at all funky and then I passed it off by making a joke.

Shortly afterwards, in May 1915, the 24th Battalion London Regiment took part in the Battle of Auber Ridge. Garner-Smith depicted the opening of the battle in a letter home:

> The sun was shining and it was a beautiful Sunday morning. The Shrapnel bursting all over the place was very exciting … Four battalions on our left had orders to get across to the German trenches in front of them … Well they got quite close to the German parapet, when a German battery of machine guns, which our artillery had missed, opened on them. They went down like corn …

On 25 May 1915 Garner-Smith's battalion was again involved in an attack. At first the attack made progress, advancing some 400 yards but in the evening they were caught by a heavy German artillery bombardment in which Garner-Smith was mortally wounded. It is clear that his father decided to spread the news of the war to the then neutral American public by releasing a number of his private letters home to the press because they were extensively quoted in the report of his death published in the *Brooklyn Daily Eagle*, the local newspaper in the neighbourhood where his parents then lived in New York.

Garner-Smith has no known grave but is commemorated on Le Touret Memorial, France, and a plaque in the College Chapel. The Garner-Smith family also endowed a school prize, the Garner-Smith Cup, which is still awarded every year to the outgoing Head of School.

Top: *Photographs of Eric Garner-Smith belonging to his descendant, Nancy Garner-Smith Myers.*

Above: *Memorial plaque to Eric Garner-Smith, in Brighton College Chapel.*

Corporal Frank Hewes Keddell (Durnford 1906–1907)

Killed in action, France, 8 June 1915 (aged 23)

Frank Keddell was born in Essex on 24 October 1891. He was the only son and second child of Harry Keddell, an oil merchant, and his wife Eleanor (*née* Hatfield). While at the College for a year he was a member of the OTC. After leaving school Keddell emigrated to Canada on the SS *Teutonic* in 1912, where he became an electrician in Toronto.

Shortly after the outbreak of war, in November 1914, he volunteered for service with the 15th Infantry Battalion CEF, which was one of three battalions raised by the 48th Highlanders, a 'Canadian Scottish' Regiment, which – despite the fact that many of its recruits had no Scottish ancestry whatsoever – wore kilts into battle. It was while serving with this unit, which formed part of Canadian 1st Division, that Keddell was killed in action on 8 June 1915, shortly after arriving in France.

Keddell's grave is in the Woburn Abbey Cemetery, France.

Lance-Corporal Henry Hatton (Junior and Hampden Houses 1899–1902)

Killed in action, Belgium, 16 June 1915 (aged 28)

Henry Hatton was born on 18 July 1886 in Bethnal Green, London. He was the youngest son and fourth child of Joseph Hatton (formerly Joseph Schwarz) and his wife Elizabeth (*née* Hart). Although details of Henry's early life are sketchy it is clear that the family had moved to 26 Daleham Gardens, Hampstead, prior to his becoming a pupil at the College. It is unclear what his occupation was after leaving the College but the indications are that he became an office worker in the City.

In 1911 Hatton enlisted with the Honourable Artillery Company (HAC), a territorial regiment based in, as it is now, the City of London. On 26 December 1914 he was attached to the 1st Battalion, HAC, which formed part of 3rd Division, on the Western Front. On 16 June 1915 he was killed in action at the Battle of Hooge (sometimes known as Bellewarde).

Hatton has no known grave but he is commemorated on the Menin Gate at Ypres, Belgium.

Top left: *Corporal Frank Hewes Keddell (BCRH).*

Top right: *Woburn Abbey Cemetery, Cuinchy, France.*

Captain John Dobree Durell Wickham
(Junior and School Houses 1892–1903)

Died of wounds, Belgium, 22 June 1915 (aged 30)

John Wickham, known as Jack, was born in Brighton on 17 September 1884. He was the elder son of Dobree Wickham, sometime housemaster at the College, and his wife Madeleine (*née* Durell). While at the College he was Captain of the football 1st XI and also played for the cricket 1st XI. On leaving the school he attended RMC Sandhurst before receiving a commission in the Lincolnshire Regiment in May 1905, becoming Lieutenant in July 1907, and Captain in May 1911. He was posted to India for five years before being seconded to the West African Frontier Force in Southern Nigeria in 1910, with whom he took part in several punitive expeditions.

On the outbreak of war he served with the Yola Column of the Expeditionary Force in the campaign against the German colony of Cameroons. However, in January 1915 he was invalided back to Britain having contracted 'black water fever'. In June 1915, after recovering, he re-joined his original unit, the 2nd Battalion, Lincolnshire Regiment, now attached to 8th Division. Shortly after his arrival in Flanders he sustained wounds while fighting near Ypres on 21 June and then died of them the following day.

Wickham has no known grave but is commemorated on the Menin Gate Memorial, Ypres, Belgium.

Above: *Brighton College football team, 1901. John Wickham is centre, with football.*

Lance-Corporal Hubert Edgar Nunn
(School House 1902–1907)

Killed in action, Turkey, 23 June 1915 (aged 24)

Hubert Nunn was born in Kent on 18 February 1891. He was the elder son of Albert Edgar Nunn, a water engineer, and his wife Frances (*née* Turner). There are a few records of Nunn's time at the College but it appears that on leaving the school he joined his father in the engineering business. By early 1910 the family was living in Marlbrook Road, Putney, London (coincidentally the exact street where the author was born) and Nunn's father was running a firm of engineers in London, A.E. Nunn and Co., while his mother appears to have been a housewife and head of the small household.

However, shortly afterwards his parents became at least partially separated, although Frances Nunn still occasionally called on Albert Nunn at his office in the City of London. On the morning of Saturday 18 July 1910 Albert Nunn was in his office but later departed for Cromer, Norfolk, then a relatively popular seaside resort, with his wife. It may be that the purpose of the holiday was to attempt a reconciliation with his wife or to keep up the appearance that they were still a family unit. Newspaper reports indicate that he arrived and registered with his wife at Cliftonville private hotel and that they appeared to be in high spirits when they retired at 11:30pm after dinner. The following day the couple did not appear at breakfast and after the Hotel Porter spotted a woman's prostrate body through the window the alarm was raised. Evidence heard at the Coroner's inquest indicated that Albert Nunn was found lying in bed in 'night attire' having been shot twice in the head at close range, while his wife Frances Nunn was lying prostrate on the floor in her dinner dress still clutching the revolver with which she had shot herself and her husband. A note written by Frances Nunn was found, which asked in vain for the story to be 'kept from the newspapers for the sake of friends and relatives who have been so kind. Say a serious accident has happened to Mr and Mrs Nunn. Please keep it from the papers for my boy's [presumably Hubert's younger brother Reginald's] sake.' The explanation which she gave for the same note indicates that she perpetrated the murder-suicide because she thought her husband was an adulterer: 'how many broken hearts at home might be spared if only the 7th commandment could be dealt with as the 6th and 8th are.' Whether the Coroner's subsequent verdict, that there was no foundation to her suspicions about her husband and that she was in fact a 'lunatic not of sound mind', was correct will never be known.

Hubert Nunn then moved to Wales, where in 1911 he was apparently working as a water engineer himself. Not much further is known about his life prior to the outbreak of war, except that his younger brother was living nearby in Wales and was also an engineer. Following the outbreak of war Hubert enlisted in the small Engineers section of the Royal Marines. He was promoted to Lance-Corporal on 28 December 1914. The Royal Marines formed a large proportion of the force known as the Royal Naval Division, which was composed of naval

Above: *Lance-Corporal Hubert Edgar Nunn (BCRH).*

personnel fighting as infantry. As might be expected, given the amphibious nature the Royal Naval Division, it was at the forefront of the Gallipoli campaign, which started in April 1915. On 23 June 1915 it appears that Nunn died of wounds sustained the same day during heavy raids on the Turkish trenches.

Nunn's grave is in the Skew Ridge Cemetery, Gallipoli, Turkey.

Lieutenant Edward Arnold Dyer (School House 1888–1890)

Killed in action, Turkey, 28 June 1915 (aged 41)

Edward Dyer (known as Arnold) was born in Alton, Hampshire on 22 July 1873. He was the eldest son and first child, of six, of Edward Dyer, a builder, and his wife Annie (*née* Brinton). While at the College Dyer was a member of the 3rd XI but was academically undistinguished. On leaving the school he was articled to a firm of solicitors in London and appears from the 1891 Census to have resided in Biggleswade, Bedfordshire, before moving to south-west London. In 1896 he qualified as a solicitor and around 1900 became a Partner in the firm of Dalbiac, Dyer and Co. In 1905 Dyer married Barbara Simpson, a pianist, and in 1907 they had a son, Arnold Erskine. The following year Dyer dissolved his London Partnership and the family emigrated to Canada where he again practised as a lawyer in Calgary, Alberta. In parallel with his legal career Dyer had a varied and significant part-time military career. He joined the HAC in 1894 and then joined the City of London Volunteers in January 1900 to fight in the Boer War. After 11 months' service Dyer received a commission as a Lieutenant in the Imperial Yeomanry, a territorial cavalry unit, with whom he took part in several actions during the closing stages of the war during the winter of 1901/1902.

Despite his age, Dyer joined the Canadian Expeditionary Force on the outbreak of war. However, for reasons unclear, he did not stay in the Canadian forces but transferred to the 9th Battalion, Shropshire Light Infantry as a Lieutenant in January 1915 and was then attached to the 1st Battalion Border Regiment for the Gallipoli Campaign. While with the Border Regiment he was killed in action during the costly but successful attack on 'Boomerang Redoubt' in Gully Ravine, where hitherto the British forces had gained on average a few feet of territory every day since the first landings in April, on 28 June 1915.

Dyer's grave is in Twelve Tree Copse Cemetery, Helles, Turkey.

Above: *Lieutenant Edward Arnold Dyer. Unit: 9th Battalion, King's Shropshire Light Infantry, attached to 1st Battalion, Border Regiment.*

Captain Alexander Gonclavez Glenday
(Hampden 1898–1904)

Died of wounds, France, 8 August 1915 (aged 27)

Alexander Glenday was born on 3 September 1887 in Sutton Coldfield, Warwickshire. He was the eldest son of Reverend Edward Alexander Glenday, and his wife Marie (née Gonclavez). Relatively little is known about Glenday's career at the College, except that during the period the family lived in Tunbridge Wells. After leaving the College, Glenday went to RMA Woolwich and received a commission in the Royal Engineers in 1907 and was promoted to Captain in 1914.

After the war began he was attached to 21st Company, 3rd Sappers and Miners, which formed part of 3rd Lahore Division (Indian Army) in France. It was customary for technical units such as Engineer Companies to be seconded directly from the British Army to the Indian Army. In August 1915 the Lahore Division was in the line in France having played a part in the Battle of Festubert in May, and having suffered heavy casualties the previous winter. The circumstances of Glenday's death are unclear, with some records stating that he died of wounds and others saying that he was killed in action but it is clear that on or around 8 August 1915 Glenday was recorded as dead and an attempt was made to inform his next of kin, who was his brother Roy in East Africa.

Glenday's grave is in the Cabaret-Rouge British Cemetery, Souchez, France. Administrating his estate was clearly particularly difficult and there are several instances of creditors, including tobacconists and Cox and Kings Bank, claiming money that he owed to them from the India Office. His youngest brother, Ferdinand Glenday OB, was also killed in the war. His two other brothers, Roy and Vincent, became, respectively, a distinguished economist and colonial administrator.

2nd Lieutenant Aubrey William Fyldes
(Chichester House 1911–1914)

Killed in action, Turkey, 9 August 1915 (aged 18)

Aubrey William Fyldes was born in Hartington, Derbyshire on 14 February 1897. He was the younger son and third child of Reverend William Fyldes and his wife Amy (née Lynde). By the time Fyldes was a pupil at the College, about which there are few records, his family had moved to Lancashire.

Following the outbreak of the First World War Fyldes enlisted in the East Lancashire Regiment and, after officer training, received a commission. He was attached to the 4th Battalion, part of 42nd Lancashire Division, which was sent to Helles on the Gallipoli peninsula in May 1915 to reinforce and attempt to extend the bridgehead made by the ANZAC Corps in late 1915. On 9 August 1915 Fyldes was killed in action while holding the line in a static position at Helles. Fyldes's grave is in the Redoubt Cemetery, Helles, Turkey.

Lieutenant Philip Clarence Williams
(Chichester 1908–1913)

Killed in action, Turkey, 10 August 1915 (aged 21)

Philip Williams was born in Brighton on 9 May 1894. He was the second son of Harry Williams, a solicitor, and his wife Harriette (*née* Kuhe). While at the College he played cricket for the 1st and 2nd XIs and was a sergeant in the OTC. He was also clearly academically successful because after leaving the school in 1913 he matriculated at Merton College, Oxford.

Shortly after the outbreak of war, on 1 September 1914, rather than returning to Oxford for a second year, he received a commission as a 2nd Lieutenant in the 10th Battalion, Hampshire Regiment, and was promoted to Lieutenant in early 1915 as the army continued to expand. The following year the 10th Battalion took part in landings at Suvla Bay in August 1915 where, on 10 August 1915, just five days after the initial landing, Williams was killed in action.

Williams has no known grave but is commemorated on the Helles Memorial, Gallipoli, Turkey.

> IN LOVING MEMORY OF
> PHILIP CLARENCE WILLIAMS,
> 2nd LIEUT. HAMPSHIRE REGIMENT,
> WHO WAS KILLED AT SUVLA BAY, GALLIPOLI
> AUG 10th 1915.

Opposite: *2nd Lieutenant Aubrey William Fyldes (BCRH).*

Top: *Chichester House, 1913, when Aubrey Fyldes attended.*

Above left: *Philip Williams as a member of Brighton College cricket team, 1913.*

Above right: *Memorial plaque to Philip Williams, in Brighton College Chapel.*

Major Henry George Watkin (Wickham's 1886–1891)

Died of wounds, Turkey, 21 August 1915 (aged 41)

Henry George Watkin was born in Tunbridge Wells, Kent on 18 August 1874. He was the eldest son and second child of Major Henry Watkin (Indian Army) and his wife Sophia (*née* Annette). Very few records exist of Watkin's life at the College but it is clear that he left to become a professional soldier who was originally commissioned into the 4th Hussars. In 1902 he was married to Evelyn, who lived in Stawley, Somerset, but was born in India, and whose maiden name has thus proved untraceable. In later life Henry Watkin listed his address as 92 Onslow Gardens, Kensington, Middlesex, London.

In August 1915 Watkin was serving as 'Brigade Major' (i.e. Chief of Staff) in the 2nd South Midland Mounted Brigade, a yeomanry cavalry brigade that took part in the landings at Suvla Bay, Gallipoli. In mid-August 1915 the brigade was commanded to dismount in order to reinforce the lines of the newly formed bridgehead at Suvla Bay. It was there that during the Battle of Scimitar Hill on 21 August 1915 Watkin was wounded and died of his wounds later the same day.

Watkin has no known grave. It is possible that he was buried at sea after being evacuated to a hospital ship lying offshore, but he is commemorated on the Helles Memorial, Gallipoli, Turkey.

2nd Lieutenant Dennis Carlton Blyth (School House 1909–1911)

Killed in action, Belgium, 28 August 1915 (aged 22)

Dennis Carlton Blyth was born in 'Refrullic' [probably a misspelling of 'Republic', or Argentine Republic, on the 1901 census transcript], Argentina, on 8 April 1893. He was eldest of five children of Alfred Blyth, who worked on the Argentine Railways and eventually rose to be Chief Clerk, and Frances Blyth (*née* Rolls). In 1901 the family returned to England and lived briefly in St Albans but shortly afterwards they moved back to Argentina. At the time Argentina was what would now be called an 'emerging market', the economy of which was the fastest growing in the world, driven by exports of refrigerated meat to European markets and large-scale British investment, especially in the railway network, which was entirely British run. Blyth's father Alfred received the CBE for his services to British commercial interests, which is noteworthy because, despite Britain's huge influence and economic interests in Argentina in the early 1900s, it was still an independent state not a colony and his position was purely commercial rather than official. Despite his family's return to Argentina, Blyth was educated in England, first at Christ's Hospital between 1907 and 1909, and then at the College. In both schools he was a member of the OTC but, unlike some of his fellow pupils and future officers, did not rise above the rank of private. After leaving the College he returned briefly to Argentina before commencing a degree in Engineering at University College, London in 1913.

On the outbreak of war he enlisted in the Royal Engineers and rapidly received a commission as a 2nd Lieutenant in 93rd Field Company, Royal Engineers in September 1914, which was attached to 17th (Northern) Division. As a territorial division the 17th was initially allocated to home defence duties but the growing demand for more troops meant that in July 1915 the division was sent to France.

On 28 August 1915, shortly after his arrival in France, Blyth was leading a 'wiring party' which was constructing an advanced field telephone network at night to connect a newly built front-line trench with the headquarters in the rear. However, the covering patrol from the 12th Manchester Regiment, which was supposed to screen the party from the enemy while it carried out its work, was not as far forward as it should have been. Despite having noticed this, Blyth took the courageous decision to carry on with his work and complete the telephone network before daybreak. However, despite the cover of darkness, the party was overheard by an enemy listening post and Blyth, along with some others, was shot and killed.

Blyth's grave is in the New Military Cemetery, Dickebusch, Belgium.

Gunner Walter Martin (School House 1909–1911)

Killed in action, France, 13 September 1915 (aged 22)

Walter Martin was born on 24 August 1893 in Lincolnshire. He was the 4th son of Frank Martin, a farmer and land agent, and his wife Violet (née Smith). Martin initially attended De Aston School in Market Rasen, Lincolnshire, but then – like two of his three brothers before him – went to Brighton College in 1909. While at the school he was an accomplished footballer, described in the report for the 1st XI as 'Neat with his feet and a fairly sound tackler'. He was also a member of the 'Playground Committee' and a Lance-Corporal in the OTC. He was presented with a prize for Mathematics in 1911, thus escaping the Dean of Chichester's acerbic comment at Speech Day that year that 'God [must be] very fond of the commonplace boy, because he had made so many of them.' After leaving the school he became an engineer's assistant with Black Sluice Commissioners (an agricultural engineering and drainage firm).

On the outbreak of war Martin enlisted in the 1st North Midland Brigade, Royal Field Artillery, which was attached to 46th Division. The division was heavily involved in the Loos offensive in September 1915, during which he was killed in action. The letter sent by his commanding officer to his parents gave the following description of his death and character:

Above: *Walter Martin as a member of Brighton College football team, 1910.*

... your son Gunner Walter Martin was killed in action on the 13th inst. at 2:40pm. He had just been told to send a signal and had taken his stand at the same moment a 5.9 inch shell dropped on the gun pit about six yards from him. He and two other telephonists, as well as two gunners in the gun pit, were killed instantaneously, and we have buried him just where it occurred ...

He was of sterling quality ... and [it] would seem to be almost a double loss in that his name had been sent forward for a Commission.

Martin has no known grave but is commemorated on the Loos Memorial, France.

Top: Books given to Walter Martin as prizes from Brighton College, and postcards from Martin to his family.

Above: British troops advance to the attack through a cloud of poison gas, as viewed from the trench which they have just left. Photograph taken by a soldier of the London Rifle Brigade on the opening day of the Battle of Loos, 25 September 1915.

2nd Lieutenant Alan Flavell Ventris
(Hampden 1910–1914)

Killed in action, Belgium, 14 September 1915 (aged 18)

Alan Ventris was born in Ootacamund, India on 15 December 1896. He was the younger son and third child of Major General Francis Ventris and his wife Helen. In 1902 on Major-General Ventris's retirement the family left India and moved to Hastings, Sussex and in 1908 again to Brighton where from 1910 Ventris was educated at the College.

On the outbreak of war Ventris underwent officer training, after which he received a commission in the South Lancashire Regiment, and was attached to the 2nd Battalion, which formed part of 3rd Division. In September 1915 3rd Division was involved in the attack on Bellewaerde near Ypres, in support of the Loos offensive. On 14 September 1915 Ventris's platoon faced a German counter-attack in which its trench appeared likely to be overrun. Ventris gave the order to evacuate and was the last to leave the trench, but as he turned down the communication trench a German grenade exploded just behind him, killing him instantly.

Ventris's grave is in Birr Cross Roads Cemetery, Ypres, Belgium.

2nd Lieutenant Alan Emilius Young
(School House 1905–1913)

Killed in action, France, 25 September 1915 (aged 20)

Alan Young was born in Bangor, Wales on 8 July 1895. He was the 3rd son of Emilius Alexander Young, a quarry and shipping manager for Lord Penrhyn, and Eliza Young (*née* Matthews). Young's father was a tough businessman, who during a strike by South Wales quarrymen from 1900–1903 in protest at attempts to prevent them forming trade unions, brought in contractors to do the strikers' work. Some strikers were then physically assaulted and were represented in the subsequent court case by David Lloyd-George. After his father's death in 1910 the family moved to 13 Morden Road, Blackheath, London. However, it is unclear why Emilius and his older brother Leslie attended the College because it preceded the family's move to London by some years and at least one of the

Top: *Ventris family grave in Hastings Cemetery, including a memorial to to Alan Flavell Ventris.*

other brothers went to Wellington College instead. At the College Alan Young was a Fives player of considerable repute; indeed his Junior House Fives team were judged 'far superior to any of the others'. Reports on his cricket were less positive, with one report stating that 'Young [can] hit very hard and straight, but has no defence. Rather slow in the field.' In his final year Young was made a school prefect.

Shortly after the outbreak of war he volunteered for the army and on 14 March 1915 he received a commission as a 2nd Lieutenant in the London Regiment and was attached to 20th Battalion, London Regiment (Blackheath and Woolwich), which formed part of 47th Division. It was as part of this unit that he was involved in the first day of the Battle of Loos on 25 September 1915. As one of the units involved in the initial assault 20th Battalion, London Regiment suffered losses of 9 officers and 162 men, among whom was Young, who, having initially been declared missing, was later declared dead.

Young has no known grave but he is commemorated on the Loos War Memorial, France. His older brother Leslie Young OB was also killed in the war (see page 70).

2nd Lieutenant Bryan Barton Cubitt (Chichester House 1906–1910)

Killed in action, France, 26 September 1915 (aged 23)

Bryan Barton Cubitt was born in Norfolk on 11 May 1892. He was the only son and eldest child of Bernard Cubitt, a gentleman farmer, and his wife Helen (née Barton). The College records indicate that he was a skilled and passionate cricketer who not only played for the school but also for Norfolk County Cricket Club. After leaving school he joined his father on the farm and is listed in the 1911 Census as a poultry farmer and 'employer'. It is clear that the farm was involved in more than just poultry, indeed it was probably predominantly arable, and so it may be that Bryan Cubitt had started a nascent poultry business, which was a relatively new aspect of farming at the time.

On the outbreak of war Bryan Cubitt received a commission in the 8th Battalion East Yorkshire Regiment formed as one of Kitchener's 'New Battalions' on 22 September 1914. After a fairly prolonged period of training, during which it appears that Cubitt was promoted to Lieutenant, the battalion landed at Boulogne on 9 September 1915. The battalion's first action was the Battle of Loos on 25 September 1915, in which the assaulting battalions suffered heavy losses, but despite this the British attempted to sustain the attack the following day, during which Cubitt was killed in action.

Cubitt has no known grave but is commemorated on the Loos Memorial, France.

Above: Bryan Cubitt in the Brighton College cricket team, 1909.

Private Kenneth Charles Goodyear
(Durnford House 1906–1909)

Killed in action, France, 28 September 1915 (aged 25)

Kenneth Goodyear was born on 24 August 1890 in Bromley, Kent. He was the only child of Thomas Goodyear, a chartered accountant, and his wife Lizzie (*née* Kedell). There are few records of Goodyear's time at the College but he was evidently academically successful because he subsequently went up to Magdalen College, Oxford, to read Mathematics, graduating with a 1st-class degree in 1914. He was also a noted young photographer, who had exhibited his photographs in London.

On the outbreak of war Goodyear, instead of training to be an officer (possibly for reasons of conscience) volunteered for service with the RAMC ambulance service. He was posted to 3rd Division Field Ambulance unit and arrived in France on 16 January 1915 as part of 85th Field Ambulance Company. While on home leave, later in 1915, he married Nancy Martin. He was killed instantly by enemy shellfire while stretcher-bearing at Vermelles during the Battle of Loos, on 28 September 1915.

Goodyear is buried in Barts Alley Cemetery, Loos, France. His father paid a significant amount for a memorial window in the extension of the College Chapel, depicting St Joseph, St Peter, St John and a pelican – a symbol included in the Brighton College crest.

TO THE GLORY OF GOD AND IN LOVING MEMORY OF KENNETH CHARLES GOODYEAR KILLED AT VERMELLES SEPTEMBER 28TH 1915 WHILE SERVING IN THE R.A.M.C. WHOSOEVER WILL BE CHIEF AMONG YOU LET HIM BE YOUR SERVANT. MATT 20.27

Top: *Private Kenneth Charles Goodyear (BCRH).*

Above: *Memorial window to Kenneth Goodyear, in Brighton College Chapel.*

2nd Lieutenant Edward Ernest Vaile
(Chichester House 1905–1907)

Killed in action, Belgium, 5 October 1915 (aged 24)

Edward Vaile was born in Essex on 18 June 1891. He was the second son, of four, of Philip Vaile, a lace manufacturer of French descent, and his wife Amy (*née* Gilbert). The family later moved to Regent's Park, London where they belatedly had a daughter, Amy. Vaile was a pupil at the College alongside his two brothers, one of whom, Philip, was also killed in the war (see page 90). On leaving the College he became a legal clerk in a London chambers. Between 1906 and 1914 it appears that he also joined up and later received a part-time commission in the HAC, a territorial unit.

Shortly after the outbreak of war in 1914 Vaile was transferred to 3rd Battalion, Worcestershire Regiment, a county with which he may have had family connections on his mother's side. In early October 1915 the battalion manned the trenches at Sanctuary Wood near Ypres, then a relatively quiet stretch of the front, during which the battalion suffered very slight losses. However, Vaile was among them, being killed in action on 5 October 1915.

Vaile has no known grave but is commemorated on the Menin Gate, Ypres, Belgium.

Major Walter Fitz-Alan Stewart
(Hampden 1890–1891)

Died of wounds, Great Britain, 3 November 1915 (aged 42)

Walter Stewart was born in Umballa, West Bengal, India on 18 August 1872. He was the youngest son of Anthony Stewart, a Colonel in the Indian Army who was one of the Stewarts of Ardvorlich, Scotland, and his wife Charlotte (*née* Barlow). By 1881 the family, although not Stewart's father, were resident in Preston, Sussex, which may explain why Stewart was subsequently a pupil at the College. On leaving school Stewart received a commission in the Indian Army on 3 September 1892 and it is probable that from then until the outbreak of the war he was based in India.

It appears that on the outbreak of war Stewart may have accompanied the Indian Expeditionary Corps to Europe, where he received wounds on the Western Front before being invalided back to Britain. He died while staying with a friend in Long Ashton, Somerset, on 3 November 1915.

Above: *Edward Vaile during his time at Chichester House, 1906.*

2nd Lieutenant Herbert Morice Lewis
(Junior, Durnford and Hampden Houses 1907–1913)

Killed in action, Turkey, 4 November 1915 (aged 20)

Herbert Lewis was born in Caythorpe, Lincolnshire, on 29 December 1894. He was the youngest son and third child of Reverend Edward Lewis, Rector of Caythorpe, and his wife Margaret (*née* Rowsell). After a successful career at the College he went up to Clare College, Cambridge. At the end of his first year the war broke out and he volunteered for the Public Schools Battalion in September 1914. He then received a commission in the Middlesex Regiment on 22 April 1915.

After further training in Britain he volunteered for service at Gallipoli and was attached to the 10th Battalion, Middlesex Regiment, which formed part of 53rd Division, in September 1915. The battalion had suffered badly during the landings at Suvla Bay in early August and had acquired, whether fairly or not, a poor reputation as a combat unit. As a result the unit was mainly confined to fatigue duties, rather than the front-line, over the following two months. Nonetheless, Lewis was killed in action on 4 November 1915.

Lewis has no known grave but is commemorated on the Helles Memorial, Gallipoli, Turkey.

Top: *2nd Lieutenant Herbert Morice Lewis (BCRH).*

Above: *Helles Memorial, Gallipoli, Turkey.*

Sergeant Edward Victor Welch
(Hampden House 1905–1907)

Killed in action, Mesopotamia, 22 December 1915 (aged 26)

Edward Welch was born in Kingston, Surrey on 14 December 1889. He was the third son and fourth child of Major Howard Welch, a professional officer who died while a prisoner of war in October 1915, and his wife Minnie (*née* Jourdain). While Welch was a child his family moved from London to Hove and after completing his education at the College he enlisted in the 2nd Battalion, Hampshire Regiment, with whom he did tours of duty in South Africa and Mauritius, and in 1914, India.

Following the outbreak of war Welch's battalion landed at Gallipoli on 25 April 1915. It is unlikely, however, that he served there because at some point following the outbreak of war he was detached from his battalion and posted to the Supply and Transport Corps serving with the expeditionary force in Mesopotamia. It was there that Welch died on 22 December 1915.

Welch has no known grave but is commemorated on the Basra Memorial, Iraq.

Above: *Sergeant Edward Victor Welch (BCRH).*

Left: *The Welch family home in Patcham, Surrey.*

Opposite top: *Edward Welch (back row, third from right), as a member of the Brighton College cricket team, 1907.*

Opposite bottom: *The Basra Memorial in its original location.*

1916

Trench warfare on the Western Front during the First World War.

Lieutenant Charles William Turton
(Hampden House 1907–1911)

Accidentally killed, Great Britain, 4 February 1916 (aged 21)

Charles Turton (also known as Cecil) was born in Brighton on 1 April 1894. He was the youngest son and third child of James Turton, a doctor, and his wife Ellen. Turton entered the College in 1907, won a prize for French in summer 1910 and on leaving the school in 1911 his family made a small contribution towards the renovation of the Chapel.

After the outbreak of war Turton undertook officer training and received a commission in the Royal Sussex Regiment. It appears that he did not take part in any front-line service before being killed in a motorcycle accident in Rottingdean, Sussex on 4 February 1916 while still attached to the 3rd (depot) Battalion, Royal Sussex Regiment.

Turton's grave is in Brighton Extra-Mural Cemetery, Brighton, Sussex.

Corporal Leslie Furmston Evans
(Junior House 1902–1903)

Died of wounds, Belgium, 16 March 1916 (aged 19)

Leslie Evans was born on 28 March 1896 in East Dulwich, Surrey. He was the younger son and second child, of five, of Henry Evans, a stockbroker, and his wife Florence (née Wright). The circumstances of Evans's life, such as where he was educated after the College, are very unclear but it appears that he emigrated to Canada on reaching adulthood.

On the outbreak of war he enlisted in the ranks of the 21st Battalion (East Ontario), Canadian Infantry, later being promoted to Corporal. It was with this unit that he sustained wounds while fighting in the St Eloi area of Belgium and died following medical complications on 16 March 1916.

Evans's grave is in Ridge Wood Military Cemetery, Ypres, Belgium.

Top: *Lieutenant Charles William Turton (BCRH).*

Left: *Corporal Leslie Furmston Evans (BCRH).*

Opposite top: *Lieutenant Reginald William Reade (BCRH).*

Opposite bottom: *2nd Lieutenant Alfred Henderson Webb (BCRH).*

Lieutenant Reginald William Reade
(Chichester House 1905–1911)

Killed in action, Mesopotamia, 5 April 1916 (aged 24)

Reginald Reade was born on 14 December 1891 in Wolverhampton, Staffordshire. He was the fifth child and youngest son of Thomas Reade, who owned a successful pharmaceuticals business producing products such as 'Reade's Egyptian Salve', and his wife Elizabeth (*née* Tozer). Reade was a scholar at the College who in his last year won the Latin Prize as well as being a school prefect and a Sergeant in the OTC. He was also a noted sportsman, who played cricket for the College's 1st XI and football for the 1st VIII Fives team, and a keen debater. (He argued in one debate that 'Socialism is to be welcomed because it is extreme and it is only by the constant struggle of extremes that progress is made'.) In 1911 he went up to Emmanuel College, Cambridge to read Classics, from which one report by a fellow OB stated that 'Reade ... is turning hermit and spends his time with ancient philosophers', indicating that he was destined for an academic career.

The war broke out very shortly after his graduation from Cambridge and, although he had been offered a post as a Classics master at Glenalmond School, Reade immediately volunteered for officer training. On 23 February 1915 he received a commission in the 9th Battalion Warwickshire Regiment. While attached to the 9th Warwickshires he was wounded at Gallipoli and invalided home but returned to his unit in January 1916. In February he arrived in Mesopotamia and he was then killed in action on the night of April 4/5 1916.

Reade's grave is in Amara War Cemetery, Maysan, Iraq.

2nd Lieutenant Alfred Henderson Webb
(Hampden House 1904–1912)

Died of wounds, Mesopotamia, 4 May 1916 (aged 22)

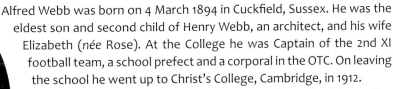

WEAVER, Pte. G., 3237. 40th Brit. Gen. Hosp. Royal Army Medical Corps. 15th July, 1917. IV. F. 3.

WEBB, 2nd Lt. Alfred Henderson. 3rd Bn. Leicestershire Regt. 4th May, 1916. Age 23. Son of H. P. H. and Elizabeth Webb, of 78, Dyke Rd., Brighton. Native of Hurstpierpoint, Sussex. III. L. 10.

WEBB, Lce. Cpl. B., 49082. 2nd Garrison Bn. Northumberland Fusiliers. 22nd Oct., 1918. I. R. 11.

Alfred Webb was born on 4 March 1894 in Cuckfield, Sussex. He was the eldest son and second child of Henry Webb, an architect, and his wife Elizabeth (*née* Rose). At the College he was Captain of the 2nd XI football team, a school prefect and a corporal in the OTC. On leaving the school he went up to Christ's College, Cambridge, in 1912.

On the outbreak of war he enlisted in the Public Schools' Battalion but after being transferred for officer training received a commission in the 3rd Battalion, Lancashire Regiment in 1915. He was later transferred to the 2nd Battalion, Lancashires, which was one of the three British Battalions attached to 7th (Meerut) Division, Indian Army, in Mesopotamia. He was killed in action there on 4 May 1916.

Webb's grave is in Basra War Cemetery, Iraq.

Captain Leslie Alexander Young (School House 1905–1908)

Killed in action, France, 21 May 1916 (aged 25)

Leslie Alexander Young was born in Bangor, North Wales on 3 June 1891. He was the eldest son of Emilius, a business manager for Lord Penrhyn, and his wife Eliza. Initially Young and his brothers were educated in Cheshire but in the 1900s the family moved from Wales to Kidbrook and Young and his younger brother Alan, who was also killed in the war, were sent to the College (see page 59). After leaving the College Young became an articled clerk in an accountancy practice and lived in Blackheath, London. In April 1913, he married Amy Petrie, sister of J.A. Petrie, an Old Brightonian.

On the outbreak of war Young initially enlisted with the 20th (Blackheath and Woolwich) Battalion, London Regiment, a locally based territorial unit. Following the expansion of the army Young put himself forward for officer training and received a commission in the same unit. Following heavy fighting at Festubert and Loos in 1915 Young was promoted to Captain. On 21 May 1916 Young was killed while defending against a major German attack in the Vimy Ridge area intended as a 'spoiler' for the expected British Summer offensive, which materialised on the Somme in July 1916. The circumstances of his death were described as follows by one of his fellow officers:

Leslie was in the front trench at the time the Bosches attacked it ... and those of us who were there know what he did ... [an interestingly oblique reference]. His Company went up into the trenches on Saturday night over 60 strong. I brought out 16 in the early morning the following day.

Young's grave is in the Cabaret Rouge Cemetery in Souchez, France. On 25 September 1916 his wife Amy bore him a son (stillborn).

Midshipman William Llewelyn Griffith (Junior House 1905–1910)

Killed in action, Battle of Jutland, 31 May 1916 (aged 18)

William Griffith was born in Brighton on 15 July 1897. He was the third son and youngest child of Arthur Griffith, a solicitor, and his wife Caroline (*née* Hall). After being a member of Junior House at the College Griffith, unusually for a Brightonian, went straight to the Royal Naval College Osborne, Isle of Wight, aged thirteen.

When war broke out he received a commission as a Midshipman and was immediately posted to HMS *Doris* and afterwards

Top: *Captain Leslie Alexander Young (BCRH).*

Left: *Midshipman William Llewelyn Griffith (BCRH).*

HMS *Glory*, both old cruisers based in Halifax, Nova Scotia, for the purposes of defending merchant shipping from German raiders in the North Atlantic. In 1915 HMS *Glory* moved to the Eastern Mediterranean where it assisted in the evacuation of British and Australian troops following the failure of the Gallipoli campaign in December 1915. In April 1916, Griffith returned to England on leave and was then transferred to the battlecruiser HMS *Indefatigable*, which he joined on 25 April 1916. On 31 May 1916 HMS *Indefatigable* was one of the battlecruisers in Admiral Beatty's squadron that engaged the German fleet at the start of the Battle of Jutland. Griffith was killed in action when, in the early stages of the battle, *Indefatigable* received a direct hit on one of her magazines from a shell fired by the German battlecruiser *Von der Tann*.

Griffith is commemorated on the Plymouth Naval Memorial. The wreck of the HMS *Indefatigable* is a designated war grave lying off the Danish coast in the North Sea.

Above: *The British battlecruiser HMS* Indefatigable *sinking after one of her magazines was hit by shellfire from the German battlecruiser SMS* Von Der Tann, *the resulting explosion then destroying her.*
All but two of Indefatigable's *crew of 1,119 were killed in the blast.*

Captain Leslie Woodroffe MC
(Junior House 1894–1898)

Died of wounds, France, 4 June 1916 (aged 30)

Leslie Woodroffe was born in Lewes on 17 October 1885. He was the second son, of four, of Henry Woodroffe, a wine merchant, and his wife Clara (née Clayton). After attending the College for four years he went to Marlborough to complete his education, being elected a senior scholar there in 1900. In 1904 he went up to University College, Oxford, where he took a Second Class Degree in Classics in 1908.

He then became an Assistant Master at Shrewsbury School in 1909, where he remained until the outbreak of war. In December 1914 he received a commission in the 8th Battalion, Rifle Brigade, attached to 14th (Light) Division. During 1915 he was awarded the Military Cross for his gallantry in action at Hooge, where he was severely wounded. Woodroffe's younger brother Sidney, who did not attend Brighton College, won a posthumous VC in the same battle. After a prolonged period of recovery, during which he returned briefly to Shrewsbury, he was promoted to Captain and returned to the front, where he died of wounds sustained in combat on 4 June 1916.

One of the five Shrewsbury masters who survived the war, out of the ten that served, was C.A. Allington, who compiled the letters they sent back to the school. There are some references to Woodroffe's death in one written by his erstwhile colleague Malcolm White, who was also killed at a later date:

> I could never have thought they would send [Woodroffe (following his earlier severe injury)] out again. He was so very much part of the place [i.e. Shrewsbury], and is still. Do you think that we all continue to have our part in the place after death? Even when not remembered?
>
> ... I expect that he [Woodroffe] met death easily; for I think he trained himself in self-sacrifice.

Woodroffe is buried in the Barlin Communal Cemetery Extension, Béthune, France. His brothers, Sidney Woodroffe VC and Kenneth Woodroffe, who both attended Marlborough College, were also killed in the war. His parents erected a memorial to all three of them in All Saints Church, Bournemouth, where they moved in later life.

Above: Photographic portrait of Leslie Woodroffe from the Marlborough College Roll of Honour.

Private Hubert Eustace King Garbett
(Hampden House 1903–1906)

Killed in action, France, 30 June 1916 (aged 28)

Hubert Garbett was born on 19 May 1888 in Cuckfield, Sussex. He was the second son and third child of Francis Garbett (a market gardener) and his wife Mary (née Clay). Garbett was at the College from 1903 until 1906, after which he entered his father's gardening business in Sussex.

Shortly after the outbreak of war Garbett enlisted in the Royal Sussex Regiment and was in due course posted to the 13th Battalion, which landed at Le Havre, France, on 14 March 1916 and was, along with two other Royal Sussex battalions, attached to 39th Division. On 30 June 1916, the day before the start of the main Somme offensive, 39th Division was ordered to mount a diversionary attack in the Richebourg L'Avoué area to the north of the Somme, which became known as the Battle of Boar's Head. Owing to the delayed start of the main Somme offensive the Germans had been able to prepare their defences and as a result 349 officers and men of the Royal Sussex were killed, including Garbett.

Garbett's grave is in St Vaast Post Military Cemetery, Richebourg L'Avoué, France.

2nd Lieutenant Basil Henry Belcher
(Junior and Chichester Houses 1905–1911)

Killed in action, France, 1 July 1916 (aged 22)

Basil Belcher was born on 3 August 1893 in Newbury, Berkshire. He was the second son and youngest child of William Belcher, a solicitor, and his wife Mary (née Miles) and the nephew of Rev Thomas Belcher, Head Master of the College, whose sons Raymond, Gordon and Harold were also killed in the war. After leaving the College he studied for a period in Paris and in summer 1914 was about to travel to Russia for further study.

However, when war broke out he enlisted in the Public Schools Battalion (18th Battalion, Royal Fusiliers) but was later selected for officer training and received a commission in the Royal Berkshire Regiment on 16 May 1915. Belcher was later attached to the 2nd Battalion Royal Berkshire, which formed part of 8th Division on the

Top: *Private Hubert Eustace King Garbett (BCRH).*

Above: *2nd Lieutenant Basil Henry Belcher (BCRH).*

first day of the Somme offensive, 1 July 1916. As soon as it went over the top his platoon ran into heavy machine-gun fire and Belcher was reported missing after being seen to fall soon afterwards. His Colonel wrote:

> He was a very good boy indeed. When he joined I told him that if he came up to the standard of his cousin [Captain Gordon Belcher MC], he would do right well. I think I can say in truth that he came up to that standard.

After the war Belcher's body was retrieved and his grave is in Serre Road Cemetery No. 2, Beaumont-Hamel, France. Belcher's paternal first cousins Raymond Belcher OB, Gordon Belcher OB and Harold Belcher OB were also killed in the war.

Major George Sutherland Guyon (Mr Wickham's House 1886–1891)

Killed in action, France, 1 July 1916 (aged 41)

George Sutherland Guyon was born in Hastings, Sussex on 19 January 1875. He was the son of Major-General Gardiner Guyon and his wife Mary (née Sutherland). After he left the College there are few details of Guyon's life, although clearly he must have received some officer training, probably at RMC Sandhurst, before he received a commission in the Royal Fusiliers, in 1897. He fought with the 2nd Battalion Royal Fusiliers in the Boer War and was promoted to Captain in 1901. He then continued to serve in the Royal Fusiliers for the next thirteen years, particularly in India, achieving the rank of Major in 1912. In preparation for his promotion he undertook a staff officer's course at the Staff College, Camberley, during which time he met his future wife Winifred (née Ryan). They were married in 1909 and returned to India shortly afterwards, where the first of their two sons, John, was born in 1910.

At the outbreak of war Major Guyon was Commanding Officer of the 2nd Battalion, Royal Fusiliers, attached to 29th Division, which was composed of British troops based in India and did not arrive in the European theatre until early 1915, when it was despatched to the planned Gallipoli campaign. A sheaf of Guyon's letters written from the troopship SS *Alaunia* prior to the landing is in the Imperial War Museum's Collection. During the landing at X Beach on Cape Helles, Guyon received a bullet wound to the head but made a full recovery. George Pierie, the battalion MO, makes several mentions of Guyon in his diary; these indicate that he had both the degree of *sang-froid* required of a battlefield commander and a very good sense of humour, apparently referring to the flimsy barricade that protected their positions as the 'rabbit hutch'.

Above: *George Sutherland Guyon aged 5.*

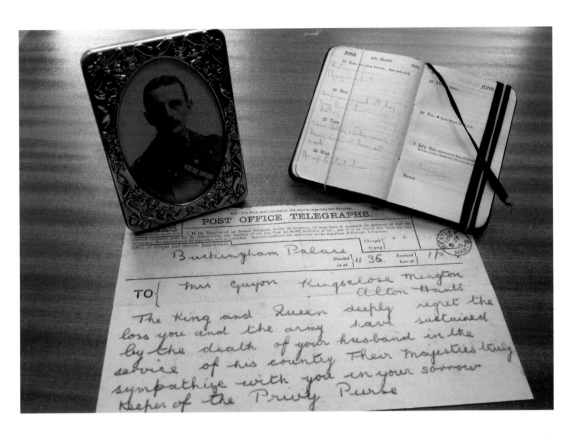

Following the evacuation of Gallipoli, after spending a short period with his family in England, he was promoted to acting Lieutenant-Colonel and given command of one of the famous 'Pals' battalions, which formed part of Kitchener's New Army – the 16th Battalion West Yorkshire Regiment (1st Bradford Pals). The battalion was attached to 31st Division and was given the objective of capturing the village of Serre on the opening day of the Somme offensive, 1 July 1916. However, German machine guns raked the communication trenches where Guyon and his troops were waiting to go 'over the top'. Guyon received another wound in the head, which rendered him instantly unconscious and, although he was bandaged up by a Lieutenant Laxton, he died shortly afterwards. During the attack that followed the battalion did not achieve any of its objectives. After his death George Pierie wrote in his diary that Guyon was *'my O.C. at Gallipoli and a nicer man never lived'*.

Guyon has no known grave but is commemorated, using his temporary rank of Lieutenant-Colonel, on the Thiepval Memorial, Somme, France.

Top: Guyon's last known portrait, his diary open at 1st July, and the 'Kings & Queen's' telegram which broke the news of his death to his wife.

Above: Guyon's 1916 diary somehow made it back from the battlefield to his family.

Captain Spencer Henry Jeudwine
(Junior House 1906–1909)

Killed in action, France, 1 July 1916 (aged 20)

Spencer Jeudwine was born in Grantham, Lincolnshire, on 22 October 1895. He was the youngest of eleven children of Reverend George Wynne Jeudwine, the Rector of Harlaxton, Lincolnshire, and his wife Harriet (née Phelps). Jeudwine entered the College aged 11 and was apparently an academic pupil, being commended for the effort he put into the library and coming second in his form in 1909. In that year he left the College to complete his education at Malvern College, where he won a number of science prizes and was accepted for a place at Gonville and Caius College, Cambridge.

However, following the outbreak of war in summer 1914 he deferred his place at Cambridge and received a commission in the Lincolnshire Regiment. While serving with the 2nd Battalion Lincolnshire Regiment, attached to 8th Division, he was promoted to Lieutenant in February 1915, received a minor wound in May 1915 and was promoted again to Captain in March 1916. A series of letters sent by Jeudwine to his sister reveal a lot about both his character and the life of a junior officer in the trenches. One shows that he had to rely on private parcels from home for vital trench equipment like periscopes and that even in a quiet sector of the front line he could only expect 2 hours' sleep in every 24. Another indicates that army candles were both expensive and very smelly and in a context where they were using up three or four a night they needed 'home-growns' to supplement army supplies. Finally there is the revelation that he deliberately avoided meeting his father on his departure from Victoria Station after what was to be his last home leave because he clearly felt it would be too traumatic.

At the Somme on 1 July 1916 the 2nd Lincolnshires were instructed to attack the German-held village of Ovillers-la-Boisselle. The regimental diary records that between 7:30am and 7:50am they succeeded in taking control of a 200-yard stretch of the first German line despite intense machine-gun and rifle fire, which made an attempt to press on to the second line impossible. Their flanks were also open to attack, particularly by grenades, from the Germans still holding trenches on either side. As a result they were forced to withdraw from the gains they had made by 9am. The battalion had sustained 450 casualties, including 21 officers. Among the officer casualties reported as 'missing' was Jeudwine.

Jeudwine has no known grave but he is commemorated on the Thiepval Memorial, Somme, France. In addition, he is depicted in a large stained-glass window in what was his father's church – St Mary and St Peter, Harlaxton, Lincolnshire.

Above: *Captain Spencer Henry Jeudwine (BCRH).*

Captain Gerald Tassel-Neame MC
(Junior House 1896–1899)

Killed in action, France, 1 July 1916 (aged 31)

Gerald Neame was born on 28 April 1885 in Horewood, Surrey. He was the eldest son and first child of Frank Neame, who owned a sugar refinery in McNade, Australia, and his wife Louisa (*née* Bennet). At the College Neame distinguished himself both on the sports field – playing football and cricket for the Junior XI – and academically, winning the Latin and German prizes. In 1899 Neame went to Cheltenham College to complete his education and thereafter lived by 'his own means', indicating that the family, who owned the famous brewery in Kent, was by 1911 very wealthy.

On the outbreak of war Neame received a commission in the 7th Battalion, East Kent Regiment ('the Buffs'), a New Army unit attached to 18th Division, and was posted to France in July 1915, being promoted to Captain in late 1915. While on leave in early 1916 he married Phyllis Bell on 27 February 1916, in what was described in the local newspaper as a 'fashionable marriage'. On the first day of the Somme campaign, 1 July 1916, he took part in the assault on Montauban. The 7th Buffs suffered heavy losses early in the initial assault and, although its attack had been relatively successful, Neame's company, which had been held in reserve, was required at midday to take the final German positions. It was in the course of this engagement, in the early afternoon, that Neame was killed in action and awarded a posthumous Military Cross.

Neame's grave is in Delville Wood Cemetery, Longueval, France. Four of Neame's first cousins – Geoffrey Neame OB, Raymond Belcher OB, Gordon Belcher OB, and Harold Belcher OB – were also killed in the war.

Top: *Captain Gerald Tassel-Neame MC (BCRH).*

Above: *Imperial War Graves Commission record showing details of Gerald Neame's headstone.*

2nd Lieutenant Theodore Wilson Chalk
(Hampden 1897–1903)

Killed in action, France, 3 July 1916 (aged 30)

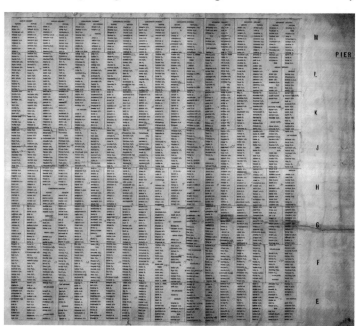

Theodore Chalk was born in Brighton on 29 January 1886. He was the youngest son and fourth child of John Chalk, a solicitor who died just before he was born, and his wife Beatrice (*née* Ellis). While at the College he was a noted Fives player, representing the school in a national competition in 1900 and also played for the 2nd XI football and 3rd XI cricket teams. In 1903 he became both a school prefect and a corporal in the OTC. It is unclear what Chalk did after leaving the College, although both he and his mother evidently moved to Kensington, London. It is likely that Chalk then spent some time abroad, as he was absent from the country for the 1911 Census.

Chalk did not immediately volunteer on the outbreak of war, another indicator that he may have been abroad, but received a commission in the Suffolk Regiment in September 1915. He was attached to the 7th Battalion, part of 12th (Eastern) Division. The division was moved forward to relieve the assault divisions on the Somme on the night of 1 July 1916 and attempted to continue the disastrous attack on Ovillers-la-Boisselle through a night attack. Although the attack was initially successful, the 7th Suffolks carrying two lines of German trenches, it later got bogged down in the face of intense German fire. At some point during the aftermath of this attack, on 3 July, Chalk was reported missing and never seen again. The Grant of Probate given to his mother in 1919 simply states that he died 'on or after 3 July 1916'.

Chalk has no known grave but is commemorated on the Thiepval Memorial, Somme, France.

Top: *2nd Lieutenant Theodore Wilson Chalk (BCRH).*

Above: *A memorial panel list, which includes Theodore Chalk.*

Captain Lister Durell Wickham
(Chichester House 1908–1913)

Killed in action, France, 3 July 1916 (aged 21)

Lister, known as Ben, Wickham was born on 25 February 1895 in Brighton, Sussex. He was the youngest child of Dobree Wickham, housemaster of the College's Junior House, and his wife Madelaine (*née* Durrell). Wickham was a pupil at the College long after his father had retired and moved to Crowborough, Sussex. At the College Wickham played for the 1st XI football team, the team report stating that although he had 'very little natural skill at the game' he had 'made himself useful by sheer hard work' and was a Sergeant in the school OTC and a school prefect. After leaving the College he worked in London for The Borneo Company, which oversaw mining and mineral exploration in what is now Sarawak, Malaysia and in February 1914 joined the Inns of Court OTC.

On the outbreak of war Wickham received a commission in the 6th Battalion, Lincolnshire Regiment, which, after training on Salisbury Plain, embarked for Gallipoli on 30 June 1915. Having fought with the battalion for three weeks Wickham contracted dysentery and on 29 July was invalided home. After some months' recovery and further time on 'general duties' at home, presumably staffing the Lincolnshire's regimental depot, he

Top: *Lister Wickham in the Brighton College football team, 1912.*

Above: *Harry North with Jane Philipson, a living descendent of Lister Wickham. Jane Philipson kindly donated Wickham's medals to the school.*

Above right: *Lister Wickham's medals.*

married Marguerite Dickinson, a musician and professional singer, in Grantham on 10 May 1916, before returning to active service. He was promoted to Captain and attached to the 7th Lincolnshires, which formed part of 17th Division. After preliminary training the battalion was moved to Morlancourt on 30 June and, along with the rest of 17th Division, took part in the first day of the Somme offensive the following day. The battalion was initially held in reserve but was ordered into action in the evening of 1 July 1916 and occupied Fricourt with relatively little loss the following day. However on 3 July, Wickham's command, A Company, 7th Lincolnshires, was ordered to take part in an attack on 'Crucifix Trench' near Mametz. The attack was, overall, quite successful by the standards of the Somme offensive as 600 Germans were taken prisoner in exchange for only 180 British casualties. However, after suffering a minor leg wound at the start of the action Wickham was killed by machine gun fire two hours later, just as the enemy position was being taken.

Wickham has no known grave but is commemorated on the Thiepval Memorial, Somme, France. In addition, his widow Marguerite, who later remarried, commemorated him by adopting 'Lister' as her stage name. His elder brother, John ('Jack') Wickham, was also killed in the war.

Captain Gilfrid Montier Reeve (School House 1902–1905)

Killed in action, France, 8 July 1916 (aged 27)

Gilfrid Montier Reeve was born on 6 December 1888 in Walthamstow, London. He was the only son and second child of Gilfrid Reeve, a brewer, later based in Essex, and his wife Alice (née Montier). After attending the College Reeve became an actuary and an expert advocate of Bimetallism. Bimetallism is the theory that there should be a fixed ratio of value between gold and silver, a pertinent issue in the era of the Gold Standard when the value of all major currencies was fixed to gold. Following a major speech he gave in 1911 advocating the use of a bimetallic standard he was admitted as a Fellow of the Institute of Actuaries in 1912.

When war broke out he received a commission in the Essex Regiment and was initially attached to the 12th (Reserve) Battalion before being later transferred to the 9th Battalion for overseas service. It was with the 9th Battalion that he took part in an attack on Ovilliers during the first phase of the Battle of the Somme. The attack began on 4 July 1916; sometime thereafter, probably the next day, Reeve was reported missing, although the College has 8 July 1916 recorded as his date of death.

Reeve has no known grave but is commemorated on the Thiepval Memorial, Somme, France, and on the War Memorial at the Institute of Actuaries.

Major George Eric Venner (School House 1905–1909)

Killed in action, France, 8 July 1916 (aged 24)

George Venner was born on 28 November 1891 in London. He was the only son and third child of John Venner, a veterinary surgeon and his wife Emily (*née* Baxter). It is clear that in 1911 he was living, if only temporarily, with his grandfather, a wealthy ex-Naval Captain called Charles Edwin Venner, in Arlingham, Gloucestershire. After leaving the College in 1909 Venner immediately underwent officer training and then received a commission in the Nottinghamshire and Derby Regiment ('Sherwood Foresters'). In 1912 he was posted with the 1st Battalion, Sherwood Foresters to Bombay, India. In India he met Margaret Dawson, who had connections with India, whom he was later to marry in Farnham, Hampshire in spring 1916.

On the outbreak of war the 1st Battalion, Sherwood Foresters was withdrawn from India and sent to France, where it formed part of 8th Division from November 1914. After taking part in the battles of Neuve Chappelle and Loos, Venner was promoted to Major on 2 December 1915. During the following summer the 1st Sherwood Foresters participated in the opening attacks of the Somme offensive. It was during such an attack, on Trones Wood near Contalmaison, that Venner was killed in action on 8 July 1916.

Venner's grave is in Dantzig Alley British Cemetery, Mametz, France and his name can be found on a memorial plaque in the College Chapel.

Bombardier Ralph Kendall Wickham (Wickham's 1885–1892)

Killed in action, Belgium, 9 July 1916 (aged 41)

Ralph Wickham was born in Compton, Hampshire, on 29 March 1875. He was one of fourteen children of Reverend Charles Wickham, parish priest of Compton and also briefly a housemaster at the College, and his wife Clara (*née* de Havilland). Wickham's life after he left school is unclear, although embarkation records indicate that in 1902 he left Britain to visit his brother's family in Australia, and that he was employed as a book-keeper, which was the occupation he entered for himself in the passenger manifest. Sometime afterwards he moved to Canada and was living there when war broke out in 1914.

Above, left: *Major George Eric Venner (BCRH).*

Above, right: *Memorial plaque to Eric Venner in Brighton College Chapel.*

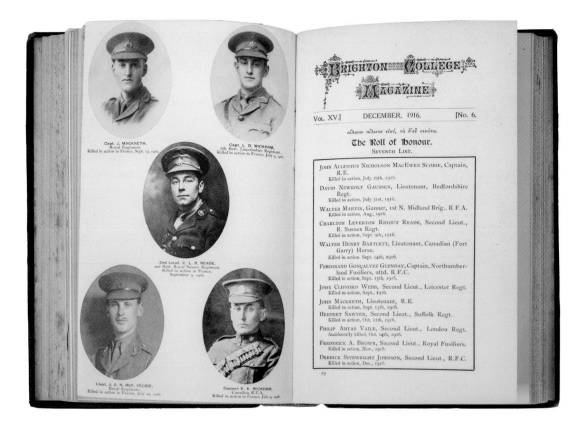

On 22 September 1914 he enlisted in the Canadian Army and was posted to the 1st Brigade Canadian Field Artillery. After crossing the Atlantic in October 1914 and undertaking a period of training in Britain the unit arrived in France on 11 February 1915 and, along with the rest of the Canadian Corps, took up a position near Ypres. On 9 July 1916 Wickham was killed when his battery was attacked by enemy aircraft east of Zillebeke in the direction of Mount Sorrel.

Wickham's grave is in the Bedford House Cemetery, Ypres, Belgium. Two of Wickham's nephews, John and Lister Wickham, both attended the College and lost their lives in the war (see pages 51 and 79).

Lieutenant John Angus Nicolson McEwen Scobie (Hampden House 1909–1912)

Killed in action, France, 29 July 1916 (aged 21)

Scobie was born in Berar, India, on 3 September 1894. He was the elder son of Donald Scobie, an engineer with the Indian Public Works Department, and his wife Joan (née McEwen). In 1900 his mother died in Toungoo, Upper Burma, and shortly thereafter the family moved to Hove where they lived with Joan's sister Mary McEwen. There are few other details about his early years and his time at the College available.

Above: *Obituaries to John Scobie and Ralph Wickham in The Roll of Honour published in the* Brightonian Magazine, *December 1916.*

Given his father's profession it is unsurprising that at the outbreak of war he enlisted in the Royal Engineers, rather than an infantry regiment, although his younger brother later chose to join the Royal Garrison Artillery. During 1915 Scobie received a commission in the 225th (Stockton-on-Tees) Company, Royal Engineers, which was sent to France in February 1916. The unit suffered heavy losses during the battle of the Somme, during which it was brigaded with several battalions of the Sussex Regiment. Among these losses was Scobie, who was killed in action on 30 July 1916, while involved in heavy fighting on the banks of the River Ancre.

Scobie's grave is in Le Touret Commonwealth War Cemetery, Richebourg L'Avoué, France. Scobie's only brother, Keith Scobie OB, was also killed in the war (see page 144).

Lieutenant David Newbold Gaussen
(Junior House 1903–1904)

Killed in action, France, 31 July 1916 (aged 23)

David Gaussen was born on 25 July 1893 in Liverpool. He was the eldest son and third child of Reverend Charles Edward Gaussen, who described his occupation as 'curing souls', and his wife Mary. After spending a brief period at the College his family moved to Herefordshire and completed his education at Berkhamsted School. He then went up to Oxford where he was President of the Oxford University Athletics Club and represented the British Universities in a 4 × 1 mile relay team, which beat the American Universities by a foot in a competition that took place in Spring 1914.

Following the outbreak of war he received a commission in the Bedfordshire Regiment and was attached to the 1st Battalion, which formed part of 5th Division. During the Somme campaign he sustained wounds on 30 July 1916 during the Battle of Delville Wood and died from his wounds the next day.

Gaussen's grave is in Dernancourt Communal Cemetery, Dernancourt, France.

Top: *Lieutenant John Angus Nicolson McEwen Scobie (BCRH).*

Above: *Lieutenant David Newbold Gaussen (BCRH).*

2nd Lieutenant George Harry Thornton Ross (Junior and Hampden Houses 1900–1903)

Killed in action, France, 9 August 1916 (aged 31)

George Ross was born on 30 June 1885 in Marylebone, London. He was the only son and third child of Harry Ross, a former police superintendent in Madras, and his wife Lena (*née* Battye). The family then moved to Hove, Sussex where Ross was a pupil at the College. Ross's career after leaving the College is unclear but there is the suggestion that he went abroad, presumably somewhere in the British Empire.

On the outbreak of war in 1914 he volunteered for service and received a commission in the Essex Regiment on 23 April 1915. Ross was attached to the 13th Battalion, Essex Regiment, which formed part of 2nd Division and landed in France in November 1915. Ross was listed as missing in action on 9 August 1916, during the Somme campaign. His battalion had launched an attack on Trones Wood but found that the barbed wire in No Man's Land had not, as promised, been cut so they were, in the words of the regimental diary, 'mown down by machine gun fire'.

Ross's body was later found and his grave is now in the Delville Wood Cemetery, Longueval, France.

Top: *Imperial War Graves Commission record showing details of David Gaussen's headstone.*

Above: *2nd Lieutenant George Harry Thornton Ross (BCRH).*

2nd Lieutenant Maurice Frisch
(Chichester House 1909–1911)

Killed in action, France, 25 August 1916 (aged 22)

Maurice Frisch was born on 21 December 1893 in Croydon, Surrey. He was the youngest son and fourth child of George Frisch, an architect, and his wife Gertrude. While Frisch was a child the family moved to Littlehampton in Sussex. Frisch was accordingly enrolled at the College, where he was a keen member of the 1st XI cricket team.

His occupation after he left school is unclear but on the outbreak of war he followed his brothers into the armed forces. Accordingly, after a period of officer training, he received a commission in the Rifle Brigade. In September 1915 Frisch was attached to the 2nd Battalion, Rifle Brigade, part of 8th Division. Almost a year later, on 25 August 1916, Frisch was reported missing while fighting in the Loos area.

Frisch has no known grave but he is commemorated on the Loos Memorial, France. His three elder brothers, who were pupils at Whitgift, were also killed in the war.

Charlton Leverton Ridout Reade
(Hampden House 1913–1915)

Killed in action, France, 9 September 1916 (aged 18)

Charlton Reade was born on 7 November 1897 in East London, Cape Colony, South Africa. He was the eldest child and only son of Reverend Edward Reed, a missionary, and his wife Mary (*née* Macleod). Within three years his family had returned to England and settled in Whitefield, Kent, probably because the outbreak of the Boer War made South Africa too dangerous for a young family. The 1911 Census reveals that the family, now with a maidservant aged 18, had moved to 19 College Road, Brighton, in very close proximity to the school. Reade was accordingly enrolled

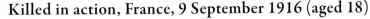

Top: *Maurice Frisch in the Brighton College cricket team, 1909.*

Left: *Charlton Leverton Ridout Reade (BCRH).*

at the College to finish his education when he was 16, although his time at the school appears to have been undistinguished. After leaving he immediately commenced officer training and received a commission in the Sussex Regiment on 6 April 1916 and was attached to the 2nd Battalion, which formed part of 1st Division.

The Sussex Regiment was heavily involved in the Battle of the Somme, including the last stages of the famous 'Battle for High Wood'. It was there that Reade was killed in action on 9 September 1916.

After the battle it appears that Reade's body was never formally identified and was buried in an unmarked grave. Reade is accordingly commemorated on the 'Special Memorial' at the Regina Trench Cemetery, Grandcourt, France.

Lieutenant Walter Henry Bartlett (Junior and Hampden Houses 1888–1896)

Killed in action, France, 14 September 1916 (aged 38)

Walter Bartlett was born in Croydon on 29 May 1879. He was the second son and third child (of nine) of Reverend Charles Bartlett, vicar of All Saints, Brighton, and his wife Mary Ann (née Eastty). Not much is recorded about Bartlett's time at the College but he was evidently an academic success because in 1896 he went up to St John's College, Cambridge, to read Law. However, possibly because of financial problems, he left before taking his degree. After leaving Cambridge he was briefly an articled clerk with a firm of solicitors in Brighton. However, it is clear that he later changed career completely because by 1911 he had emigrated to Canada where he was serving as a civil engineer with the Manitoba Hydrographic Survey Board. While in Canada he

was also heavily involved in the Scout movement, winning the Silver Wolf Medal for his services to the movement as Provincial Secretary to the Boy Scouts in Manitoba.

Bartlett enlisted in the Fort Garry Horse in May 1915 before transferring to the Canadian Infantry. He departed for Europe on the SS *Olympic* (sister ship to the *Titanic*) on 2 April 1916 and was posted to the 27th Battalion CEF, which formed part of 2nd Canadian Division, on 7 July 1916. His first

Above, left: *Lieutenant Walter Henry Bartlett (BCRH).*

Above, right: *Medal belonging to Walter Bartlett.*

action was the Battle of Flers-Courcelette in September 1916 (see the entry below for further information). However, on the evening of 14 September 1916, the day before the battalion was due to attack, Bartlett lost his life. The report of his death stated tersely that:

> This officer was killed while crawling from the front line to the 'jumping off' trench prior to the attack. He only lived for one minute after being hit and was unable to speak.

Bartlett has no known grave but his name is commemorated, along with the names of 11,000 other Canadians, on the Vimy Memorial, France. The Memorial Cross sent to his family on his death is now in the Brighton College Archive.

2nd Lieutenant John Clifford Webb (Junior and Hampden Houses 1904–1912)

Killed in action, France, 14 September 1916 (aged 21)

John Webb was born on 27 February 1895 in Cuckfield, Sussex. He was the youngest son and third child of Henry Webb, an architect, and his wife Elizabeth (*née* Rose). At the College Webb was in the Junior School for four years before entering Hampden House in September 1908. He was in the 1st VIII Fives team, as well as being a House Prefect and a Lance-Corporal in the OTC. It is unclear what he did immediately after leaving school, but shortly after the outbreak of war he volunteered for service.

In May 1915 he received a commission in the Leicestershire Regiment and was later attached to the 1st Battalion Leicestershire Regiment in France, part of 6th Division. The 6th Division played a prominent role in the later stages of the Battle of the Somme, taking part in the Battle of Flers-Courcelette, in which tanks were used, albeit ineffectively, for the first time. It was there that starting on 15 September 1916 four days of attacks were made by 6th Division on a strong German position, known as the 'Quadrilateral Redoubt'. Webb was killed in action on the first day while attempting to move through the German wire at the head of his platoon. His company commander wrote following his death that:

> He was killed … at the head of his men, most of whom were killed with him by a machine gun hidden in a shell hole in front of the German line. He was killed instantaneously, and was actually within a few yards of the enemy position when he fell.

Webb's grave is in the Guards' Cemetery, Lesboeufs, France. Webb's brother, Alfred Webb OB, was also killed in the war (see page 69).

Above: *2nd Lieutenant John Clifford Webb (BCRH).*

Captain Ferdinand Gonclavez Glenday
(Hampden House 1900–1903)

Killed in action, France, 15 September 1916 (aged 24)

Ferdinand Glenday was born on 9 January 1892 in Aston, Warwickshire. He was the youngest son and sixth child of Alexander Glenday, an import and export merchant, and his wife Marie (*née* Lopes). Marie Lopes died aged 31 and in 1903, when Ferdinand was only 11, his father also died. He and his siblings were taken in by his uncle, Reverend Edward Albert Glenday, Rector of Holy Trinity Church in Bury, Lancashire. After the family moved to the North he became a pupil at the prestigious Manchester Grammar School and from there went up to Keble College, Oxford, in 1911 to read Modern History.

Following the outbreak of war he received a commission in 12th Battalion Northumberland Fusiliers and was rapidly promoted to Captain. In the regimental history he is referred to as 'Uncle Glenday', which gives some idea of his character as perceived by others. He was wounded at the Battle of Loos, after which he transferred to the 70th Squadron RFC. On 15 September 1916 he was acting as an observer in a Sopwith Strutter piloted by Captain C.K. Cochran-Patrick when he was killed in action. Captain Cochran-Patrick was unhurt. A patrol from the 70th Squadron, then based at Fienvillers aerodrome, was over Bapaume in the Somme area when it met a formation from Jasta 2 (an elite German fighter unit). The action is vividly described in *An Airman's Outings* by Alan Bott:

> Two observers … [were] killed during our patrol. One of them was 'Uncle,' a captain in the Northumberland Fusiliers. A bullet entered the large artery of his thigh. He bled profusely and lost consciousness in the middle of a fight with two Huns. When he came to, a few minutes later, he grabbed his gun and opened fire on an enemy. After about forty shots the chatter of the gun ceased, and through the speaking-tube a faint voice told the pilot to look round. The pilot did so, and saw a Maltese-crossed biplane falling in flames. But Uncle had faded into unconsciousness again, and he never came back. It is more than possible that if he had put a tourniquet round his thigh, instead of continuing the fight, he might have lived.

Glenday was buried in Beauval Cemetery, Somme, France. His elder brother Alexander, also an OB, was killed a year earlier at Loos in August 1915. One of his other brothers, Sir Vincent Glenday, went onto become a colonial district commissioner and then Speaker of the East African Legislative Assembly. His portrait now hangs in the National Portrait Gallery.

Lieutenant John Mackreth (Junior and Hampden Houses 1901–1911)

Killed in action, France, 15 September 1916 (aged 23)

John Mackreth was born in Brighton on 8 July 1893. He was the elder son and first child of Edmund Francis Mackreth, a clergyman, and his wife Madeline. Some time in his youth the family moved to London. Mackreth was enrolled in the Junior House in 1901, aged only 8, before

Left: Lieutenant John Mackreth (BCRH).

graduating onto Hampden House but there are few records of his time at the College or of his career immediately afterwards, although it seems likely that he was an engineer.

On the outbreak of war he received a commission in the Royal Engineers and became attached to 41st Signals Company, which managed signals for 41st Division. He was killed in action during the Battle of Flers-Courcelette on 15 September 1916.

Mackreth has no known grave but is commemorated on the Thiepval Memorial, Somme, France.

Private Robert Gordon Melville Mitchell (Mr Wickham's House 1884–1889)

Killed in action, Belgium, 10 October 1916 (aged 41)

Robert Mitchell was born on 21 May 1875 in Calcutta, India. He was the son of Robert Mitchell and his wife Marianne. Few records survive of his time at the College but after leaving he spent a period in the Indian Civil Service, and he was admitted to the Bar at the High Court, Calcutta in 1899. In 1906 he moved to Australia where he managed an orchard in West Tamar, Tasmania, married Marion (*née* Mason) in 1913 and fathered a daughter, Rosalie, in the same year.

Although already 40 years old, Mitchell enlisted as a private in the AIF at Claremont, Tasmania, on 14 September 1915. Following the slaughter at Gallipoli the ANZACs, the main component of the AIF, were already short of men and were prepared to send abroad older volunteers who would probably have been retained for home service in the British Army. Mitchell arrived in France in December 1915 and was enrolled in 15th Battalion AIF, which, as part of 4th Australian Division, was involved in the later stages of the Battle of the Somme. After seeing action on the Somme, the division was then transferred to a relatively quiet part of the front near Ypres. Nonetheless Mitchell was still exposed to artillery fire and in early October 1916 he sustained shrapnel wounds in the legs, thigh, throat and hand, from which he died on 10 October 1916.

Mitchell's grave is in Lijssenthoek Military Cemetery, Ypres, Belgium.

Above: *Portrait photograph of Robert Mitchell, 1915.*

2nd Lieutenant Herbert Montagu Sawyer
(School House 1906–1907)

Killed in action, France, 12 October 1916 (aged 27)

Herbert Sawyer was born on 25 March 1889 in Godstone, Surrey. He was the second son and fourth child of Joseph Sawyer, an architect, and his wife Mary (*née* Evison). The family was fairly itinerant in his childhood, moving first to Caterham and then ultimately to Kenley, a village on the outskirts of the then relatively prosperous town of Croydon, where he lived in a house known as The Tower. Prior to going to Brighton College, Sawyer was a pupil at Whitgift Grammar School, now known as Whitgift School. However, he finished his education by spending one year as a boarder at the College. After school Herbert followed in his father's footsteps and became an architect, presumably being apprenticed to his father's firm because they continued to live under the same roof.

On the outbreak of war Sawyer received a commission in the 9th Battalion, Suffolk Regiment which, following its formation in Bury was moved temporarily to barracks in Shoreham, Sussex and Blackdown in Surrey. The 9th Suffolks were by 1916 attached to 6th Division, with which they fought in the Battle of Le Transloy, one of the final actions of the Somme campaign, in October 1916. On 12 October 1916 6th Division attacked on a four-mile front between Eaucourt and the Bapaume–Perrone road and advanced between 500 and 1,000 yards, in the course of which Sawyer was killed in action.

Sawyer has no known grave but he is commemorated on the Thiepval Memorial, Somme, France.

2nd Lieutenant Philip Amyas Vaile
(Chichester House 1907–1911)

Accidentally killed, France, 14 October 1916 (aged 22)

Philip Amyas Vaile was born on 27 July 1894 in Marlyebone, London. He was the third son of Philippe Vaile, a manufacturer, and his wife Amy (*née* Gilbert). The family was clearly prosperous because their address is listed as Ormonde Terrace, Regent's Park. Philip Vaile became a pupil at the College in 1907 but there are few records of his time at the school or of his profession immediately after he left. However, he was clearly interested in soldiering because he enlisted in the Honourable Artillery Company, a territorial regiment staffed mainly by City professionals and based near Liverpool Street in London.

Top: *2nd Lieutenant Herbert Montagu Sawyer (BCRH).*

After war broke out Vaile received a commission in the London Regiment. However, in 1916 he was posted as an instructor to the Central School in Le Havre. The Central School was one of many establishments across Northern France intended to improve the quality of newly arrived troops through contact with serving personnel. On 14 October 1916, while Vaile was training a contingent of Canadian troops, he was accidentally killed by the premature explosion of a grenade.

Vaile is buried in St Marie Cemetery, Le Havre, France. His brother Edward, also an OB, had been killed the previous year while serving with the Worcestershire Regiment (see page 62).

2nd Lieutenant Frederick Arthur Brown (Hampden House 1905–1907)

Killed in action, France, 13 November 1916 (aged 25)

Frederick Brown was born on 9 December 1890 in Walton-on-Thames, Surrey. He was the elder son and first child of Edward Brown, a Coal Merchant, and his wife Alice. He only spent two years at the College and afterwards completed his education at the Municipal Technical College, Brighton, where he studied mathematics and engineering. It appears that he then worked as an electrical engineer until war broke out in 1914.

On the outbreak of war Brown underwent officer training and then received a commission in the Royal Fusiliers. He was killed in action with the 7th Battalion, Royal Fusiliers on 13 November 1916 during the Battle of Ancre, which was the closing phase of the Somme campaign. His commanding officer wrote to his father that:

On the morning of the 13th inst., the Battalion with many others, attacked the German position which was strongly held with machine guns. These caused many casualties to our men, and unfortunately your brave son was hit while leading his platoon just before reaching the enemy's line.

Brown's grave is in the Ancre British Cemetery, Beaumont-Hamel, France.

Top: *2nd Lieutenant Philip Amyas Vaile (BCRH).*

Above: *Lieutenant Frederick Arthur Brown (BCRH).*

2nd Lieutenant Derrick Sivewright Johnson (Hampden 1910–1914)

Killed in action, France, 4 December 1916 (aged 21)

Derrick Johnson was born in the Cape Colony (now part of South Africa) on 3 December 1895. He was the youngest son and third child of Major (later Lieutenant-Colonel) Frank Johnson and his wife Jane. His father had a distinguished military career, which he was to resume on the outbreak of war in 1914, but he retired from the army and settled in Hove while Johnson was a child. While at the College Johnson played for the football and cricket 1st XIs and acted as Secretary for Sport, as well as being a school prefect and a Corporal in the OTC.

On the outbreak of war he undertook officer training and received a commission in the Cyclist Corps, a territorial formation, before transferring to the RFC in November 1916. Within the RFC Johnson was initially attached to the 23rd and 28th Squadrons before being briefly hospitalised following an accident in September 1916. Thereafter he was attached to the 25th Squadron, a bomber unit. He was killed in action on 3 December 1916 while returning with his squadron from a raid on German positions at Pont-à-Vendin, France. The squadron was in tight formation but Johnson's plane was shot down as a result of a near vertical dive by a German aircraft and was seen to have crashed in flames behind enemy lines.

Johnson's grave is in the Cabaret-Rouge British Cemetery, Souchez, France.

Private Harold Body (Chichester House 1905–1907)

Killed in action, Belgium, 15 December 1916 (aged 26)

Harold Body was born in Hove on 31 July 1890. He was the second son and fifth child of James Body, an England Rugby player who briefly owned the brewery which stood on the site now occupied by the College's Woolton building, and his wife Alice (*née* Indcox). James and Alice Body were married in New York in 1884 and in the late 1880s lived in Winnipeg, Canada, where James Body ran a flax oil company, before returning to Brighton by 1891. Their son Harold was born after they returned to England and, like his brothers, was a pupil at the College, where he was in the football 2nd XI and the cricket 1st XI. He also won a science prize.

After leaving school Body took a job in the Bank of Montreal's office in London and later transferred to their head office in Canada. Ten months after the outbreak of war he enlisted in Princess Patricia's Canadian Light Infantry and on 9 December 1915 joined his unit in the Ypres area. On 2 June 1916 he received a bullet wound in the back and was invalided back to Britain, where he remained until declared fit for service again on 17 July 1916. However, on 15 December 1916 he was killed in action while fighting in the Mount Sorrel area near Ypres.

Body's grave is in the Ecoivres Military Cemetery, Mont-St Eloi, France.

Top: *Derrick Johnson in the Brighton College cricket team, 1914.*

Left: *Portrait photograph of Harold Body.*

Lieutenant Robert Eric Odell
(Junior and Hampden Houses 1905–1913)

Died of wounds, France, 20 December 1916 (aged 22)

Robert Odell was born on 1 December 1894 on the Isle of Wight. He was the younger son and fourth child of Reverend Robert William Odell and his wife Mary, whose maiden name is unknown but was of Canadian origin. Soon after Eric's birth the family moved to South Hampstead in London but later, following the peripatetic career characteristic of clergymen, they moved to 1 College Terrace, Brighton, because Odell's father had become the Rector of St Matthew's Church, which was on the corner of Sutherland Road and College Terrace until its demolition in 1967.

During Odell's time at the College he played for the 2nd Fives VIII and was also in the athletics team. He served as both a Corporal in the OTC and a school prefect. In 1913 Odell went up to Christ's College, Cambridge, to read Natural Sciences and apparently expressed an ambition eventually to go into the Indian Civil Service. While at Cambridge he captained the Christ's College 2nd rowing VIII, although clearly the standard was not exceptional because it appears that in the Freshers' races his cox ran the boat into the bank. He also developed an interest in the natural world, which one of his fellow Old Brightonians gently teased him about in a report for the school magazine:

> Odell, having developed an unconquerable passion for mountain-climbing, was seen one evening climbing the roof of his college, he spends his spare time fossil-hunting.

Soon after war was declared he enlisted in the Public Schools' Battalion but was later transferred out for officer training and on 4 January 1915 Odell received a commission in the 8th Battalion, Black Watch (a Highland Regiment). The reason behind this choice of regiment is unclear, as the family history does not reveal an obvious Scottish connection. Nonetheless, the 'devils in skirts', as the Germans named them, were certainly a prestigious regiment with a fearsome reputation. After serving with the Black Watch in several campaigns Odell was wounded near Arras on 18 December 1916 and he died of his wounds two days later. A letter written by a fellow officer following his death states:

> I simply cannot express my sorrow at [Odell's] death. Not only have I lost a friend, the country and the empire have lost one of the best men I ever knew. He carried with him, I always felt, a sense of freshness and sanity that came from the lakes and moors and hills that he loved so well. And there was a hidden strength in his personality which scorned the meaner things of life … How I miss his humour and quiet but malicious sarcasm. He had a keener sense of the ridiculous than any man I know … But he took his duties seriously and was a fine leader of men.

Odell's grave is in the Habarcq Communal Cemetery Extension, France.

Above: *Lieutenant Robert Eric Odell (BCRH).*

1917

The battle of Passchendaele, July to November 1917.

Captain Harold Norris Surgey
(Hampden House 1907–1909)

Killed in action, East Africa, 3 January 1917 (aged 23)

Harold Surgey was born in Crawley Down on 6 June 1893. He was the only son and younger child of William Surgey, 'who lived on his own means', and his wife Julia (*née* Palmer). While at the College he won a Mathematics prize and after leaving the school he briefly became an article-clerk in a surveyor's practice in Brighton, although it seems probable that at some point he also left the country for service elsewhere in the British Empire.

On or shortly before the outbreak of war he received a commission in the Warwickshire Regiment and was later promoted to Captain. However, the majority of his war service took place as an attached officer with the 'Arab Rifles', who were nominally part of the famous King's African Rifles but were in fact recruited from Yemeni Arabs and formed part of the Indian Army's establishment. Surgey was killed in action on 3 January 1917 while fighting in the East African Campaign against Von Lettow-Vorbeck's 'Askaris'. In the College Archives there is a letter written to Surgey's parents by one of his senior officers describing the circumstances of his death:

> A Company of Arab Rifles to which your boy belonged was on its way to join up with a column at Inkamba. When some way from its objective, at a place called Kofi, it was attacked in thick bush by a vastly superior force of the enemy, and it was in the course of the action that ensued that your son was killed, together with the commander of the company and some ten men. Your boy met his death as a true soldier in the most noblest manner possible ...

Surgey's grave is in the Commonwealth War Cemetery at Upanga Road, Dar Es Salaam, Tanzania.

Above: *Captain Harold Norris Surgey (BCRH).*

2nd Lieutenant William Meadows Kemp
(Chichester House 1911–1912)

Killed in action, France, 28 February 1917 (aged 20)

William Meadows Kemp was born on 8 June 1896 in Wandsworth, London. He was the third son of Arthur William Kemp, a London parfumier, and his wife Kate. No records of his time at the College, or his career immediately afterwards, exist.

Shortly after the outbreak of war Kemp received a commission in the Middlesex Regiment. His service record indicates that he was attached to a number of battalions in the regiment but spent the majority of the war with the 16th Battalion. On 28 February 1917 William Kemp was killed in action in France near Sailly-Saillisel in the Somme area – the only member of the Middlesex Regiment to be killed in that area on that particular day, in what was then a quiet area of the front.

Kemp's grave is in the Sailly-Saillisel British Cemetery, France.

2nd Lieutenant John Arnold Buckland
(Durnford 1912–1915)

Killed in action, France, 1 March 1917 (aged 20)

John Buckland was born in Ilminster, Somerset, on 5 October 1896. He was the elder son of Reverend John Buckland, Rector of Whitelackington, Somerset, and his wife Agnes (*née* Kavanagh). At the College he became a school prefect in 1914 and played for the football 1st XI and the cricket 2nd XI as well as being a Lance-Corporal in the OTC. On leaving the school he received a commission in the Somerset Light Infantry.

In summer 1916 he was attached to the 7th Battalion, Somerset Light Infantry, which formed part of 20th Division, with whom he served in the front line throughout out the second half of the Somme campaign. In early spring 1917 the 7th Somerset Light Infantry advanced following the German withdrawal to the Hindenburg Line,

Top: *2nd Lieutenant William Meadows Kemp (BCRH).*

Above: *John Buckland in the Brighton College football team, 1914.*

in the course of which, on 1 March 1917, Buckland was killed by enemy shellfire. The regimental chaplain wrote to his parents:

> Your boy was one of my best friends, and such a good fellow. His brother officers and his men loved and respected him, and it will be very hard to fill his place. He did not suffer at the last. About 3 p.m. on March 1st a 5.9 shell dropped directly on the post where he was, and death was instantaneous. He is buried at the front line, and the Battalion have erected a cross to his memory.

Buckland was reburied after the war and his grave is now in the A.I.F. Burial Ground, Flers, France.

2nd Lieutenant Ronald Maynard Ross (Junior and Hampden Houses 1905–1912)

Killed in action, France, 4 March 1917 (aged 21)

Ronald Ross was born in Brighton on 28 February 1896. He was the second son of Dr Douglas Ross, a Brighton physician, and his wife Emma (*née* Daniels). There are no known records of either his time at the College or his career immediately after he left.

On the outbreak of war Ross enlisted in the Public Schools' Battalion but shortly afterwards went to RMC Sandhurst for officer training before receiving a commission in the Worcestershire Regiment. He was attached to the 1st Battalion Worcestershire Regiment, which formed part of 8th Division. Ross was taking part in a trench raid on 4 March 1917 when, according to the account written by his commanding officer:

> He was severely wounded early in the fight, but refused to leave, and continued with his men and make [sic] headway against counter-attacks all day. Towards evening, seeing a sergeant practically buried by a shell, he hastened to dig him out, and in so doing exposed himself above the parapet; he was struck by a piece of shell and killed instantly.

Ross is buried in Fins New British Cemetery, Sorel-le-Grand, Somme, France. His elder brother, William Ross OB, was also killed in the war.

Above: *2nd Lieutenant Ronald Maynard Ross (BCRH).*

Opposite top: *Lance-Corporal Bertram Hazlehurst (BCRH).*

Opposite: *Frederick Bartley in the Brighton College cricket team, 1904.*

Lance-Corporal Bertram Hazlehurst (Hampden House 1910–1913)

Died of wounds, France, 16 March 1917 (aged 20)

Bertram Hazlehurst was born on 16 June 1896. He was the only son and eldest child of George Hazlehurst, a retired Dock Manager, and his wife Mary. George Hazlehurst was descended from a famous Methodist family which owned a soap-making company based in Runcorn, Cheshire. There are few records of Hazlehurst's career at the College or his career immediately after he left.

On the outbreak of war he joined the 23rd Battalion Royal Fusiliers, formed as the first 'Sportsmen's Battalion' and sponsored by Mrs E. Cunliffe-Owen, which was attached to 2nd Division. On 16 March 1917 the battalion was involved in the pursuit following the German retreat to the Hindenburg Line, a defence line formed on the Western Front. The Germans had orchestrated the retreat very carefully and had laid numerous ambushes and booby-traps in their wake, one of which killed Hazlehurst.

Hazlehurst's grave is in the Dernancourt Communal Cemetery Extension, Somme, France.

2nd Lieutenant Frederick John Bartley (Junior and Hampden Houses 1896–1904)

Killed in action, Palestine, 26 March 1917 (aged 30)

Fredrick Bartley was born on 14 June 1886 in Great Dunmow, Essex. He was the eldest son of Frederick Bartley, a brewer and later stockbroker, and his wife Clara (*née* Randall). The family owned a holiday home in Rottingdean, Sussex, which perhaps accounts for why Bartley was a pupil at the College, although few records remain of his career there. After leaving the College he became an auctioneer in East Anglia, where his family lived at the time.

On the outbreak of war he received a commission in the 5th Battalion, Essex Regiment, a territorial unit of which he may already have been a part-time member. The 5th Essex was attached to 54th (East Anglian) Division and was despatched to Egypt in May 1915 to guard the Suez Canal against Ottoman attack. However, during the advance into Palestine in 1917 Bartley was one of nine officers in the battalion killed in action during the assault on Mansura Ridge, known as 'Green Hill' in the Battle of Gaza on 26 March 1917.

Bartley's grave is in the Gaza War Cemetery, Gaza, Palestinian Authority.

Lieutenant Sidney Stretton
(Junior and School Houses 1901–1906)

Accidentally killed while flying over the English Channel, 27 March 1917 (aged 28)

Sidney Stretton was born in Derby on 28 October 1888. He was the eldest son and second child of Benjamin Stretton, a brewer, and his wife, Frances, who had a total of seven children of whom two died in infancy. No records remain either of Sidney's time at Brighton College, or of what he did between leaving school in 1906 and the outbreak of war.

On the outbreak of war Stretton was clearly already a commissioned officer because he was later awarded the 1914 Star, only available to those who had actually fought in 1914, but it is unclear whether he was already a member of the RFC or whether he transferred later. At some point, however, it is clear that he qualified as a pilot and was attached to the 66th Squadron RFC, with which he is recorded as having been killed in a practice flight in Britain on 27 March 1917.

Despite this record the actual circumstances of Stretton's death are rather mysterious because he has no known grave and is actually commemorated in the Doullens Communal Cemetery in France, and his body appears never to have been recovered and buried. A possible reason for the discrepancy is that his plane may have crashed over the English Channel while flying between Britain and his squadron's base in France.

Alfred Sydney Borlase Schiff
(School House 1912–1915)

Killed in action, France, 9 April 1917 (aged 19)

Alfred Schiff was born on 27 November 1897 in Mayfair, London. He was the only son and eldest child of Ernest Schiff, a stockbroker, and his wife Emma (born in New Zealand). At the College Schiff played for the 1st XI cricket team in both the 1914 and 1915 seasons.

However, he left the College aged only 17 to enrol at RMC Sandhurst in summer 1915. The following year he received a commission in the 1st Battalion Rifle Brigade, which formed part of 4th Division. In April 1917 Schiff's unit was involved in the initial attack at Arras and on the 9 April 1917 he was killed in action.

Schiff's grave is in Brown's Copse Cemetery, Roeux, France.

Above: *Lieutenant Sidney Stretton (BCRH).*

Above: *2nd Lieutenant Alfred Sydney Borlase Schiff. Unit: 1st Battalion, Rifle Brigade. Death: 9 April 1917 Western Front.*

2nd Lieutenant Edmund Charles Baldwin Childe-Pemberton (Hampden House 1911–1913)

Died of wounds, France, 13 April 1917 (aged 21)

Edmund Childe-Pemberton was born on 21 July 1895 in London. He was the elder son of William Shakespear Childe-Pemberton, a noted biographer, and his wife Constance (née Lady Constance Bligh, daughter of the 6th Earl of Damley). The family's aristocratic, literary and somewhat Bohemian background is quite unusual given the predominantly professional- and business-orientated Brighton College parents in this period. Childe-Pemberton's career at the College was brief and there are relatively few records except that he joined the army immediately after leaving in 1913.

After receiving officer training Childe-Pemberton was commissioned into the 18th (Queen Mary's Own) Royal Hussars, which on the outbreak of war arrived in France on 16 August 1914 as part of 1st Cavalry Division. After initially serving as cavalry the regiment was dismounted and was kept in reserve. Following the relatively successful attack by the Canadian Corps on Vimy Ridge in April 1917, the 18th Hussars were sent forward in an attempt to exploit the success. However Childe-Pemberton was killed in action when the advance of 1st Cavalry Division was stalled on 13 April 1917.

Childe-Pemberton's grave is at Barlin Communal Cemetery Extension, Pas de Calais, France.

Lieutenant-Colonel Foster Newton Thorne (Hampden House 1893–1895)

Killed in action, Mesopotamia, 18 April 1917 (aged 36)

Foster Newton Thorne was born in Lewes on 13 May 1880. He was the only son and fourth surviving child of Joseph Thorne, a retired China merchant, and his wife Isabel (née Pryor). He was initially educated at the College and then went on to Shrewsbury. He completed officer training and received a commission in the Royal Sussex Regiment, with which he served in the Boer War, in April 1900. Between 1901 and the outbreak of war he was posted to both Africa and India and was promoted to Captain in 1910. In 1914, while still in India, he married Sylvia Amber Walker. The couple had one daughter, Vivian Sylvia, who was born in 1916.

Top: *2nd Lieutenant Edmund Charles Baldwin Childe-Pemberton (BCRH).*

Left: *Lieutenant-Colonel Foster Newton Thorne (BCRH).*

Following the outbreak of war Thorne was promoted first to Major and then to Lieutenant-Colonel in December 1915, when he was given command of the 6th Battalion Loyal North Lancashire Regiment, which formed part of 13th Division, and despatched to Mesopotamia. It was there that he was killed in action on the Adhein (now known as Adhaim) river on 18 April 1917.

Thorne has no known grave but is commemorated on the Basra War Memorial, Iraq.

Lieutenant William Oak Jay (Hampden House 1908–1912)

Killed in action, France, 25 April 1917 (aged 22)

William Jay was born in Cape Colony, South Africa on 22 March 1895 in South Africa. He was the son of Charles Jay and his wife Gertrude. Jay's mother was widowed during or just after the Boer War and the family returned to Britain to live in Hove shortly thereafter. There are few records of Jay at the College and he returned to South Africa upon leaving.

On the outbreak of war in 1914 he fought with the South African forces (exactly in which unit is unclear) which drove the Germans out of South-West Africa (now Namibia). After the completion of that campaign he returned to Britain and received a commission in the 8th Battalion, King's Own Lancaster Regiment, which formed part of 27th Division and later 3rd Division. Jay was killed in action on 25 April 1917 during the final stage of the Battle of Arras when the 8th King's Own Lancashires was involved in repulsing German counter-attacks in the Monchy-le-Preux area. In the words that one of his fellow officers wrote to his mother:

On April 25th, he was in command of 'D' Company, holding the newly captured position in front of Monchy, when a heavy shell burst in the trench near where he was standing. He was badly hit, and died almost immediately in his servant's arms. I cannot tell you how deeply we share your sorrow, or how sincerely we feel for you in this overwhelming blow. He was such a splendid officer, fearless and cool under fire, a born leader of men because he was always so considerate for them. His men loved him and would have followed him anywhere, and his death is a great loss to the Battalion.

Jay has no known grave but is commemorated on the Arras Memorial, France.

Above: *Lieutenant William Oak Jay (BCRH).*

2nd Lieutenant William Gilbert Elphinstone Clapp (School House 1910–1912)

Died of wounds, France, 29 April 1917 (aged 23)

William Clapp was born on 25 October 1893 in Sidmouth, Devon. He was the elder son and third child of Reverend William Clapp, Rector of Ashley, Stockbridge, and his wife Louisa (*née* Clack). He was educated first at Allhallows School, Honiton, Devon before finishing his schooling at the College. Thereafter he attended Harper-Adams Agricultural College in Devon and was then a pupil to a gentleman farmer near Basingstoke.

On 20 September 1916 he received a commission in the Norfolk Yeomanry, a cavalry unit, but was then attached to the Norfolk Regiment, the county's infantry regiment, in France from December 1916. On 28 April 1917 he sustained wounds leading his platoon in an attack during the Battle of Arras and died the following day at No. 41 Casualty Clearing Station.

Clapp's grave is in Duisans British Cemetery, Arras, France.

Top: *Battle of Arras, Cleaning Station, April 1917.*

Above: *2nd Lieutenant William Gilbert Elphinstone Clapp (BCRH).*

2nd Lieutenant George Mervyn Archdale
(Chichester House 1910–1915)

Died of wounds, France, 30 April 1917 (aged 20)

George Archdale was born on 14 August 1896 in London. He was the only son and eldest child of Audley Archdale, a 'gentleman', and his wife Mary. While at the College he won a scholarship to Gonville and Caius College, Cambridge to read Medicine but then deferred entry to join the army following the outbreak of war the previous year.

He received a probationary commission in the Royal Berkshire Regiment on 13 August 1915. It is unclear what he did during the following year; either he completed his officer training or he did actually go up to Cambridge for a couple of terms pending his posting abroad. In December 1916 he arrived in France and was attached to the 1st Royal Berkshire, which formed part of 2nd Division. He fought in the latter stages of the Battle of Arras and was wounded on 29 April 1917. On 30 April 1917 he died of his wounds at the No. 1 Canadian Casualty Clearing Station.

Archdale's grave lies in the British Military Cemetery, Aubigny, France.

Above: *Chichester House during George Archdale's attendance, 1913.*

2nd Lieutenant Leonard Francis Gandar-Dower
(Hampden and Chichester Houses 1903–1909)

Killed in action, France, 3 May 1917 (aged 26)

Leonard Gandar-Dower was born in Regent's Park, London on 20 June 1890. He was one of six sons of Joseph Gandar-Dower, a tea merchant and 'colonial broker', and his wife Amelia (*née* Germain). While the family were still young they moved to Brighton where Gandar-Dower attended the College. While a pupil Gandar-Dower was appointed a prefect in 1907 and a senior prefect in 1909. He also represented the school in the 1st XI for both cricket and the 1st VIII for Fives, and was a Colour Sergeant in the OTC. After leaving the College he was a partner in Edward A. Franks and Gandar. It is not clear exactly what the nature of the partnership's business was, but given the highly successful nature of his father's business, whose probate records show him to have died an extremely wealthy man, it seems likely to have been on the same lines.

On the outbreak of war he enlisted with the HAC and was in 1916 chosen by his commanding officer for officer training. He received a commission in the 2nd Battalion, HAC, and arrived on the Western Front in January 1917. On 3 May 1917 he was reported missing in action following an attack on German lines in the closing stages of the Arras offensive. It is clear from the following report by his company commander that it was his first experience of combat:

> He [Gandar-Dower] went over the top with us a few days ago, and was doing magnificently. It was his first time under fire, but he might have been an old solider by the splendid way he carried on. I fear he is killed, as the last that was seen of him was when a bomb burst at his feet.

Above: *Chichester House, 1906. Leonard Gandar-Dower is at the centre, where the photograph is damaged.*

Although the Germans did subsequently report through Red Cross channels that he had died from wounds after being captured, Gandar-Dower has no known grave. He is commemorated on the Arras Memorial, France.

Captain John Archibald Ainslie (Hampden House 1904)

Killed in action, France, 19 May 1917 (aged 29)

John Ainslie was born in Hanwell on 26 February 1888. He was the elder son and fourth child of Archibald Ainslie, a British representative with the Chinese Imperial Customs Service and his wife Margaret (*née* Murphy). The family had recently settled back in Britain after living in Australia, where Ainslie's parents were married, and China, where two of Ainslie's older sisters were born. However, they lived in Brighton while Ainslie was a pupil at the College. It is unknown what Ainslie did immediately after leaving the College but in 1911 he received a commission in the King's Own Scottish Borderers and was attached to the 2nd Battalion in Ranikhet, India. While in India he met Jean Blanche Stewart-Wilson, the daughter of Sir Charles Stewart-Wilson, a civil servant. The Wilson family later lived in Yateley Manor, Hampshire, England. On the outbreak of war Ainslie's battalion returned to Europe and initially fought at Gallipoli, after which Ainslie came to Britain on leave and married Jean Stewart-Wilson in February 1916. In words attributed to Hetty Cumnor, a parlour maid in the Stewart-Wilson household:

> In the Edwardian and Durbar carefree days, the British Raj was still in its heyday ... a young Lieutenant and the young daughter of Sir Charles ... fell in love with each other. Sir Charles held an important position in the Bombay Presidency and his parents thought their daughter too young but said if the lovers were of the same mind after a certain period permission would be given ... [After] the First World War had begun the lovers were still of the same mind [so] they were married.

Following the marriage Ainslie was posted to the Western Front and fought in the Battle of the Somme before being killed by enemy shellfire on 19 May 1917. He was posthumously promoted to Captain on the same day, possibly as a kind gesture by his commanding officer because it would increase his widow's pension. Hetty Cumnor also recalled his young wife's reaction to the return of his belongings:

> When his belongings were sent home from the war with the filth and gore of the trenches the young lady took them up to her bedroom and shut the door. After some time had passed the parents became worried and opened the door. She had fallen asleep with her arms clasped around his [Ainslie's] coat. She was carrying his child, I believe.

Ainslie's grave is in Roclincourt Military Cemetery, France. His son, also called John Archibald, was born a few months after his death.

Above: *Captain John Archibald Ainslie (BCRH).*

2nd Lieutenant Francis Morris
(Chichester House 1910–1914)

Died of wounds, France, 29 May 1917 (aged 21)

Francis Morris was born on 21 February 1896 in Ashbourne, Derbyshire. He was the youngest son and fourth child of Canon Ernest Morris, Rector of Ashbourne and formerly regimental Chaplain for the Nottinghamshire and Derby Regiment (the Sherwood Foresters), and his wife Josephine (*née* Bolton). There are unfortunately few records of his time at the College.

After he left the College in 1914 he immediately commenced officer training and received a commission as a 2nd Lieutenant in the Sherwood Foresters in July 1915. However, he later transferred to the RFC and was posted to the 3rd Squadron RFC. While flying as a pilot with the 3rd Squadron he crashed during a blizzard in the Vimy Ridge area in April 1917 and fractured both his legs, one of which was then amputated. On 29 May 1917 he went into the operating theatre but died under the anaesthetic.

Morris's grave is in the St Sever Cemetery, Rouen, France.

Captain Raymond Belemore
(Hampden House 1901–1904)

Died of wounds, France, 8 June 1917 (aged 31)

Raymond Belemore was born in Norwich on 18 May 1886. He was the only son and eldest child of Lieutenant Alfred John Belemore, a surgeon who served for a time with the RAMC, and his wife Amelia. The family moved to 95 Montpellier Road, Brighton, shortly after the children were born. Records of Belemore's period at the College are scarce and his profession after he left school is unknown but it is clear that he continued to live in Brighton, settling in Brunswick Terrace, and that some time between leaving school and the outbreak of war he married Dorothy Culler. The couple did not have any children.

Soon after the outbreak of war, Belemore received a Commission in the Connaught Rangers and served with them, firstly with the 1st Connaught Rangers in Mesopotamia and later with the 6th Connaught Rangers on the Western Front, in the course of which he was promoted to Captain. During the 1930s, an Australian Veteran's magazine called *Reveille* printed a number of articles referring to Belemore by a Captain Tom Kelsey, who had also served in Mesopotamia.

The articles build up a picture of a larger-than-life character known ironically as 'Tiny' who drank vast quantities of rum and, despite suffering from asthma, was a heavy smoker. He was also very brave:

> I watched 'Tiny' Belemore bring up the company. How the deuce the man escaped being hit, I don't know. He looked as big an elephant, and half the Turkish Army appeared to be shooting at him.

After recuperating from a particularly bad bout of asthma Belemore was given command of a company in the 6th Battalion Connaught Rangers, which took part in the assault on the Messines Ridge on 7 June 1917. He was wounded and brought to the field hospital at Ballieul, where he died of his wounds the next day.

Belemore's grave is in the Ballieul Communal Cemetery Extension, Ballieul, France.

2nd Lieutenant George Clarence Knowles (Durnford House 1914–1915)

Died of wounds, France, 10 June 1917 (aged 19)

George Knowles was born in Wood Green, Middlesex, on 31 July 1897. He was the only son and third child of Louis Knowles, a chemist, and his wife Annie (*née* Brailsford). At the College he passed the matriculation exam for London University but before taking up his place he completed officer training at RMC Sandhurst and received a commission in the 9th Battalion, Yorkshire Regiment.

The battalion formed part of 23rd Division, which took part in the assault on the Messines Ridge in June 1917, during which Knowles sustained the wounds that led to his death on 10 June 1917. A fellow officer wrote an account of his death for his father:

> You will be glad to know he died the most glorious death imaginable. He was bringing in one of his men from the open (the man had been badly wounded) when he was shot through the arm and fell. He got up again and tried to drag the man in, when he was shot through the shoulder. After a few minutes he once again tried to drag in the wounded man, when he received a bullet in the abdomen.

Knowles's grave is in the Lijssenthoek Military Cemetery, Ypres, Belgium.

Opposite top: *2nd Lieutenant Francis Morris (BCRH).*

Opposite bottom: *Captain Raymond Belemore (BCRH).*

Above: *2nd Lieutenant George Clarence Knowles.*

Lieutenant Arthur Egerton Hodge
(School House 1910–1914)

Killed in action, France, 13 June 1917 (aged 20)

Arthur Hodge was born on 9 December 1896 in Fulham, London. He was the elder son of John Hodge, a solicitor, and his wife Maud (*née* Curtis). After John Hodge's death it appears that his widow moved to Brighton, which accounts for why her son started in School House in 1910; she then moved to Devon, meaning that Hodge became a boarder in School House from 1911. At the College Hodge was a school prefect, a member of the 1st XI cricket team and an athlete.

Hodge's occupation immediately after he left the College is unclear but after undergoing officer training he received a commission in the 1st Battalion, North Staffordshire Regiment, which formed part of 24th Division, on 25 July 1916. On 13 June 1917 he was killed in action during a number of fierce German counter-attacks aimed at recapturing the high ground in the Messines Ridge area.

Hodge's grave lies in the Railway Dugouts Burial Ground, Transport Farm, Ypres, Belgium.

Top: *Durnford House, 1914. George Knowles is second row from the back, 2nd boy from the right-hand side.*

Above: *Lieutenant Arthur Egerton Hodge (BCRH).*

Captain George Harvey (School House 1892-93)

Killed in action, France, 21 June 1917 (aged 38)

George Harvey was born in Brighton on 23 June 1878. He was the younger son and third child of Frederick Harvey, a retired army officer, and his wife Catherine (*née* Sherlock). There are few records of Harvey's time at the College although it appears that after he left he trained as a solicitor. At some point thereafter Harvey moved from Sussex to Devon because it appears that from 1912 onwards he was resident in Seaton, Devon. In the year of his death, 1917, he married Gladys Harvey, who was originally from Wales but then also lived in Devon.

Following the outbreak of war in 1914 Harvey, despite his age, received a commission in the Royal Garrison Artillery. Harvey was killed in action on 21 June 1917 while serving with the 355th Siege Battery, RGA. The 355th Siege Battery was an artillery battery held some distance behind the lines and was responsible for firing very large 9.2-inch and 12-inch guns. It is unusual for someone in such a unit to be killed in action because they were positioned so far behind the lines but Harvey's death may have been the result of either long range artillery fire from similar German guns or an air attack.

Harvey's grave is in the Cambrin Military Cemetery, Béthune, France.

2nd Lieutenant Archer Steward Richardson (Durnford 1910–1911)

Killed in action, Belgium, 25 June 1917 (aged 24)

Archer Richardson was born on 20 February 1893 in Lilleshall, Shropshire. He was the only son and eldest child of Archer Richardson, a farmer and turf accountant, and his wife Dora (*née* Campbell). While at the College he was captain of the football 1st XI, came third in the open mile and competed in the quarter- and the half-mile on sports day and was a member of the gymnastics team. He also enjoyed debating, taking part in a debate on the motion 'This House Regrets the Return of the Liberals' after the results of the very contentious 'People's Budget' election of 1910. After leaving the College he went up to Gonville and Caius College, Cambridge, to read medicine.

Richardson had probably not completely qualified as a doctor when he volunteered for the army in 1915. Nonetheless, as might be

Top: *Captain George Harvey (BCRH).*

Above: *Archer Richardson in the Brighton College football team, 1910.*

expected, he joined the RAMC as Sergeant in the 44th Field Ambulance. On 3 May 1917 he received a commission and joined the 13th Siege Battalion Royal Garrison Artillery as its Medical Officer. On 25 June 1917, very shortly after his appointment, he was killed in action near Ypres. He was recommended for a Military Medal following his actions in evacuating the wounded from Delville Wood during the Battle of the Somme but it appears that a decision on whether to make the award had not been made by the time he was killed and the application was allowed to lapse.

Richardson's grave is in the Dickebusche New Military Cemetery Extension, Ypres, Belgium.

2nd Lieutenant Edgar John Gibbons Uridge (Chichester 1911–1914)

Killed in action, France, 26 June 1917 (aged 20)

Edgar Uridge was born on 21 July 1896 in Lewes, Sussex. He was the younger son of James Uridge, a retired farmer, and his wife Mary (*née* Martin). After leaving the College in 1914 it appears that Uridge may have been aiming at a legal career because he became a private in the Inns of Court OTC.

However, the following year he began officer training at the temporary RFA cadet school at Exeter. He received a commission in the RFA on 10 September 1916 and was attached to 147th Brigade RFA, which was then a unit at the disposal of GHQ BEF 1st Army, in February 1917. In March 1917 he was seconded for staff work at the brigade headquarters, rather than being attached to one of the field batteries, and in May 1917 he spent two weeks on a training course at the 1st Army Artillery School, one of a number of field training units set up by the BEF. On 26 June 1917, shortly after he returned to his unit, he was killed in action by enemy shellfire.

Uridge's grave is in the Maroc British Cemetery, Grenay, France.

Lieutenant-Colonel Harold Thomas Belcher DSO (School House 1885–1893)

Killed in action, Belgium, 8 July 1917 (aged 42)

Harold Thomas Belcher was born on 17 March 1875 in Malvern, Worcestershire. He was the first child of seven, and eldest son of Reverend Thomas Belcher, Head Master of Brighton College 1881–1893, and his wife Annie (*née* Neame). After leaving the College he went to the RMA Woolwich and thereafter received a commission in the Royal Field Artillery. During the Boer War he fought in

Above: 2nd Lieutenant Edgar John Gibbons Uridge (BCRH).

the garrison at Ladysmith and was awarded a DSO and the Queen's Medal. After further field commands from 1910–1914 he was a company commander and instructor at the RMA Woolwich, where he held, in the words of the RMA's obituary, 'original views the soundness of which have been since been proved' and invented a widely copied ranging machine.

On the outbreak of war he was again sent into the field where, apart from a brief period in hospital following a wound, he served continuously on the Western Front from September 1914 until his death. He was rapidly promoted to Lieutenant-Colonel and given command of the 52nd Brigade, RFA, attached to 9th Scottish Division, as well as being mentioned in despatches several times and awarded the Russian Order of St Anne. In January 1917 he married Ghita Slade-Powell, the widow of a fellow officer, but had no issue before he was killed in action on 8 July 1917.

His grave is in the Dickebusch New Military Cemetery, Ypres, Belgium. A stained-glass window in the chapel in the school commemorates the lives and sacrifice of Belcher and his two brothers, Raymond Belcher OB and Gordon Belcher OB. His paternal first cousin Basil Belcher OB and his maternal first cousins Gerald Tassel-Neame OB and Geoffrey Neame OB were also killed in the war. His other brother, Arthur Belcher OB, was Head Master of the College between 1933 and 1937.

Above: *Lieutenant-Colonel Harold Thomas Belcher DSO (BCRH).*

Below: *Detail of the memorial window to the Belcher brothers in Brighton College Chapel.*

Flight Officer John Frederick William Akers
(Hampden House 1912–1914)

Killed in action while flying over Belgium, 20 July 1917 (aged 19)

John Akers was born on 15 March 1898 in Bath, Somerset. He was the elder son and second child of William Akers, a surgeon, and his wife Eleanor (*née* Powell). At the College Akers was a member of the OTC but left in 1914 aged 16 to join the Territorial Force. He was initially attached to the 1/6th Cyclist Battalion, Sussex Regiment, which was stationed in Norfolk throughout the war. On 22 December 1914 he received a temporary commission aged just 16.

However, when he turned 18 Akers applied for a transfer to the RNAS and on receiving his Aviator's Certificate on 1 May 1917 was commissioned as a Flight Officer in the Royal Navy. He was attached to 4th Squadron based at Bray-Dunes and Téteghem, Northern France. The 4th Squadron was by 1917 equipped with Sopwith Camel fighters and was responsible for patrolling the skies above the Channel coasts, including behind enemy lines in occupied Belgium. On 20 July 1917 Akers was killed in action when his aircraft was shot down while flying over German-occupied Oostende.

Akers's grave is in Oostende Communal Cemetery, West-Vlaanderen, Belgium.

Captain William Stuart Ross
(Chichester House 1902–1911)

Killed in action, Belgium, 23 July 1917 (aged 25)

William Ross was born on 6 March 1892 in Brighton. He was the eldest son of Dr Douglas Ross, a physician in Brighton, and his wife Emma (*née* Daniels). While at the College Ross represented the school in the 1st XI for both cricket and football and in the 1st VIII for Fives, as well as editing the school magazine. In 1911 he went up to St Catharine's College, Cambridge, where he was a Sergeant in the OTC.

Following the outbreak of war Ross received a commission in the Border Regiment and served at both Gallipoli and in Egypt before being sent to France. On 22 December 1916 he was promoted to Lieutenant and attached to the 6th Battalion Border Regiment, which formed part of 11th Division, in the Ypres area. On 23 July 1917, while serving as Acting Captain, he was killed along with five of his men by enemy shellfire while he was conducting a Lewis gun inspection.

Ross's grave is in La Brique Military Cemetery, West-Vlaanderen, Belgium. His younger brother, Ronald Ross OB, was also killed in the war.

Top: Flight Officer John Frederick William Akers (BCRH).
Above: William Ross in the Brighton College cricket team, 1910.

Lieutenant Edward Chamberlain Nunn
(Junior and Durnford Houses 1912–1914)

Died of fever, Mesopotamia, 24 July 1917 (aged 20)

Edward Nunn was born in Calcutta, India, on 23 November 1896. He was the son of James Nunn, a merchant, and his wife Henrietta. There are few available records of either his family or his time at the College. It is, however, clear that after he left the College he immediately returned to India where he received a commission in the 119th (Mooltan) Infantry Regiment (Indian Army) in 1915.

Like much of the Indian Army his war service took place in Mesopotamia where the Mooltan Regiment was sent as reinforcements after the disastrous defeat in the Siege of Kut in 1916. It was there that, following the successful capture of Baghdad in March 1917, Nunn contracted a fever and died in a hospital in Basra on 24 July 1917.

Nunn's grave is in the Baghdad Commonwealth War Cemetery, Iraq.

Top: *Edward Nunn in the Brighton College football team, 1913.*

Above: *Durnford House, 1913. Edward Nunn is in the back row, third from the left.*

2nd Lieutenant Colin Walter Wise
(Hampden House 1906–1909)

Killed in action, Belgium, 31 July 1917 (aged 25)

Colin Wise was born on 18 February 1892 in Balcombe Road, Cuckfield, Sussex. He was the second son and third child of Walter Wise and his wife Edith (*née* Cartner). After being educated at Brighton College he was employed as a clerk by the Royal Mail Steam Company and latterly by A.M. Rothschild. In February 1910 he enlisted in the HAC, part of the newly formed territorial force, eventually rising to the rank of Sergeant.

On the outbreak of war he was mobilised but was initially retained for home service duties. However, the following year he was enrolled in the 74th Brigade RFA and saw service in Egypt and Macedonia and in March 1916 received a temporary commission in the RFA. In July 1916 he was severely injured in a riding accident and, having also contracted malaria in hospital, was invalided home to Britain. Six months later he returned to active service and was sent to France in January 1917, and was mentioned in despatches shortly afterwards. On 31 July 1917, the first day of the Third Battle of Ypres (Passchendaele), he was killed in action after his dugout received a direct hit from an enemy shell.

Wise's grave is in Canada Farm Cemetery, Ypres, Belgium.

Lieutenant Guy Stanley Gerald Hamilton
(School House 1912–1913)

Killed in action, Belgium, 1 August 1917 (aged 19)

Guy Hamilton was born on 9 December 1897 in Sydenham, Kent. He was the eldest child and only son of Robert Hamilton, who owned a linoleum business, and his wife Lilian (*née* Richer). Few records exist of his time at the College but he did serve as a Lance-Corporal in the OTC. After leaving the College he entered the legal profession as a clerk and joined the Inns of Court OTC.

In 1915, despite being only 17, he was commissioned into the Royal West Surrey Regiment and was later attached to the 1st Battalion, Bedfordshire Regiment, with whom he went to France in 1916. After being wounded he was briefly invalided home and returned to France later in 1916 with the 3rd Battalion, Royal West Surrey Regiment. He was wounded again on 9 April 1917 during the Battle of Arras but re-joined his battalion in France as an adjutant on 11 July. He then took part in the opening attack

Top: *2nd Lieutenant Colin Walter Wise.*

Above: *Lieutenant Guy Stanley Gerald Hamilton (BCRH).*

of the Third Battle of Ypres (Passchendaele) on 31 July 1917. On the evening of the following day, 1 August 1917, he was killed instantaneously by a stray shell while standing outside the headquarters dugout as his battalion was being relieved. The commander of his battalion wrote:

> His loss is most severely felt both by myself and all ranks in the battalion. He made an ideal adjutant, being fearless, hardworking, quick and most conscientious, besides having a very high sense of duty.

Hamilton has no known grave but is commemorated on the Menin Gate, Ypres, Belgium.

2nd Lieutenant Eric John Halliwell (School House 1910–1913)

Killed in action, Belgium, 11 September 1917 (aged 20)

Eric Halliwell was born on 9 October 1896 in Transvaal, South Africa, then one of the independent Boer Republics. He was the elder son of Ernest Halliwell, a noted cricketer famed for lining his wicket-keeping gloves with raw steak, and his wife Rosena (*née* Richer). He went to prep school at Haw Bank, Cheadle, Cheshire, before coming to the College, where he was a keen sportsman and a member of the OTC. After he left the College he returned to South Africa and worked in the mining industry.

On the outbreak of war he enlisted in the Transvaal Scottish and took part in the campaign against German South-West Africa. He then returned to Britain and received a commission in the 57th Brigade, RFA, with which he was wounded at Vimy Ridge in March 1916. In early 1917 he transferred to the RFC and in July 1917 started acting as an observer. On 11 September 1917 he was listed as missing after he and his pilot did not return following a mission deep behind enemy lines. A German airman subsequently dropped a message over the British lines confirming that Halliwell had been killed in action.

Halliwell was reburied after the war and his grave is now in the Moorseele Military Cemetery, Wevelgem, Belgium.

Top: *School House, 1912, when Guy Hamilton and Eric Halliwell attended.*

Above: *2nd Lieutenant Eric John Halliwell (BCRH).*

2nd Lieutenant William Rolph Botting
(Hampden House 1905–1913)

Killed in action, Belgium, 25 September 1917 (aged 22)

William Botting was born on 29 July 1895 in Brighton. He was the elder son of Dr Herbert Botting, a musician, and his wife Florence (*née* Rolph). There are few records of Botting's time at the College but after leaving school he, like his parents, pursued an interest in music. He became a Fellow of the Royal College of Organists and acted as assistant organist at St Augustine's Church, Brighton.

Shortly after the outbreak of war, however, he became an articled clerk in a London solicitors' firm and joined the Inns of Court OTC. On 26 March 1917 he received a commission in the 11th Battalion, Royal Sussex Regiment, which formed part of 39th Division. The 11th Sussex took part in several key engagements during the Third Battle of Ypres (also known as Passchendaele), including Pickem Ridge, Langemark and, in late September 1917, the assault on the Menin Ridge. On 25 September 1917 Botting was killed in action during the final assault, which succeeded in capturing the ridge.

After his death the regimental Chaplain wrote to his parents that:

> [He had] never met anyone of a more beautiful character ... Your son, amongst others, fell in the forefront of the Empire's great battle-line a gallant and a splendid fellow in the day of trial.

Botting's grave is in Tyne Cot Cemetery and he is commemorated on the Menin Gate, Ypres, Belgium.

Flight Sub-Lieutenant Bertram Denison Kilner
(Hampden House 1909–1910)

Killed while flying over the North Sea, 25 September 1917 (aged 22)

Bertram Denison Kilner was born on 5 May 1895 in Fulham, London. He was the youngest son and third child of William Kilner, a grain merchant, and his wife Frances (*née* Harington-Clyde). The family subsequently moved to Brighton, where after a brief period at the College Kilner completed his education at Eastbourne College.

Top: *2nd Lieutenant William Rolph Botting (BCRH).*

Above: *Flight Sub-Lieutenant Bertram Denison Kilner (BCRH).*

Shortly after the outbreak of war Kilner received a commission in the RNAS on 3 December 1914 and was subsequently trained both on standard biplanes, such as the Sopwith Pup, and the seaplanes launched from one of the Navy's earliest aircraft carriers, HMS *Vindex*. He is described in one report by a superior officer in the RNAS as having 'carried out all his duties in a very efficient manner … Very capable officer.' He served as a night-flying pilot at the RNAS base in Dunkirk and at Gallipoli in support of the fleet lying offshore, where he crashed and was invalided home. In 1917 Kilner returned to front-line duties with the RNAS flying seaplanes from HMS *Vindex* to intercept the Zeppelins that the Germans used for maritime reconnaissance. On 25 September 1917 at 5:30am Kilner took off in a seaplane from HMS *Vindex* to intercept a Zeppelin, which was reported to be flying off Southern Denmark, but never returned. There were, however, no reports of air combat with the Germans and his service record simply states that death occurred during 'seaplane operations in the North Sea'.

Kilner has no known grave but is commemorated on the RNAS Memorial in Chatham, Kent.

Lieutenant Bernard Alexander Powers
(Hampden House 1911–1913)

Killed in action, France, 25 September 1917 (aged 20)

Bernard Powers was born on 31 December 1896 in Wembley, London. He was the only son and second child of Alexander Powers, a schoolmaster, and his wife Blanche (*née* Bernard). In 1911 the family moved from London to a boarding house in Brighton from which Powers attended the College. There are few records of Powers's time at the College or his career immediately after he left.

Top: *Side view of HMS* Vindex, *showing the prominent seaplane hangar aft.*

Left: *Lieutenant Bernard Alexander Powers (BCRH).*

Shortly after the outbreak of war Powers received a commission in the Middlesex Regiment. At a later date he received a promotion and volunteered for service in the RFC, receiving his Aviation Certificate on 12 November 1916. He was then attached to 19th Squadron RFC based in Northern France, in which he piloted the French-built Spad biplane. He was reported missing while flying with this squadron on 25 September 1917.

Powers has no known grave but is commemorated on the Arras Flying Services Memorial, Faubourg d'Amiens Cemetery, France.

Lieutenant Francis Clement Thompson (Hampden House 1901–1907)

Died of wounds, Belgium, 3 October 1917 (aged 28)

Francis Thomson was born on 24 October 1888. He was the younger son and third child of Reverend George Thomson and his wife Mary (*née* Butlin). After Windlesham House Thomson won a scholarship to the College where, as well as being a librarian and editor of the school magazine, he was a member of the shooting team, a Sergeant in the OTC and school prefect. After school he went up to Trinity College, Cambridge, where he gained a First in the Classical Tripos and then took a post as Assistant Latin Lecturer at the University of Wales, Cardiff.

When war broke out he joined the Inns of Court OTC and on 8 April 1915 received a commission in the Royal Field Artillery. He was attached to the 59th Brigade, RFA and served with it in Gallipoli and Egypt and then France, being promoted to Lieutenant on 3 September 1917. His brigade was heavily involved in the Third Battle of Ypres (Passchendaele) and on 3 October 1917 he was wounded in action near Ypres and died from his injuries at No. 4 Casualty Clearing Station the following day. An extract from his Colonel's letter to his bereaved parents reads:

> I cannot tell you how dreadfully sorry we are …. We all liked him immensely. He was a most hard-working and exceptionally conscientious officer … Only two days ago I sent in his name recommending him for the Military Cross. Please accept my very real sympathy in the loss of your splendid son.

Thompson's grave is in Dozinghem Military Cemetery, Westvleteren, Belgium.

Above: *Lieutenant Francis Clement Thompson (BCRH).*

Lieutenant Leslie Scott (Chichester House 1898–1899)

Killed in action, Belgium, 12 October 1917 (aged 33)

Leslie Scott was born in Ryde, Isle of Wight in 1884. He was the younger son of John Allen Scott, who owned an upholstery business, and his wife Florence (*née* Cranbrook). Scott's father died in 1886 and his mother married again to Olive Gabell, a Brighton hotelier, with the result that Scott was, briefly, a pupil at the College. After leaving the College Scott became a borough surveyor who lived and worked in Brighton before emigrating to Canada in 1906.

After the outbreak of war Scott returned to Britain and received a commission. His initial unit is unknown but in 1916 he was promoted to Lieutenant and drafted into the newly formed Household Battalion. This was a unit the core of which comprised ancillary personnel from the Household Cavalry with the addition of various other drafts who were sent to serve as infantry on the Western Front. After serving in various areas of the Western Front, the Household Battalion was deployed in the assault on Poelcappelle on 12 October 1917, in the later stages of the Third Battle of Ypres (Passchendaele). During the attack, which was unsuccessful, the battalion suffered 348 casualties, including 13 officers, out of the 498 officers and men who took part. Scott was one of those registered as missing.

Scott has no known grave but is commemorated on the Tyne Cot Memorial, near Ypres, Belgium.

Top: *Lieutenant Leslie Scott (BCRH).*

Above: *Chichester House, 1898. Leslie Scott is in the front row, middle boy on the right-hand side.*

Private Hugo Campbell Bazett
(Junior House 1888–1892)

Killed in action, Belgium, 14 October 1917 (aged 38)

Hugo Bazett was born on 6 March 1879 in Newbury, Berkshire. He was the son of Alfred Campbell Bazett, a solicitor who originated from Sussex, and his wife Jane (*née* Knowles). He had at least two sisters but the census data is so unclear for the family that it indicates an intriguing degree of noncompliance, at least as long as Alfred Bazett remained alive, and there is also little known about his school career. After leaving the College, Bazett was employed as a clerk in London and in 1903 married Emily Cunningham. The couple, who had no children, then moved to Slough where Bazett was, in 1916, working as an advertisement writer.

On the outbreak of war Bazett did not volunteer for service and when conscription was introduced in 1916 he applied to the relevant local tribunal for an exemption on the basis of his wife's poor health. However, the tribunal ruled that there were no true 'dependents' in Bazett's household and denied his application. Bazett was therefore enlisted in the Grenadier Guards and was attached to the 4th Battalion, which formed part of the 3rd Guards Brigade, Guards Division. He was killed in action on 14 October 1917 during the closing stages of the Third Battle of Ypres (Passchendaele). The regimental diary's report of the day is incomplete but it appears that the battalion was subjected to an air attack while it was resting behind the line.

Bazett's grave is in the Bleuet Farm Cemetery, Ypres, Belgium. The family informed the College of his death in 1922 but his wife, surprisingly, was not granted probate until 1936. It is unclear whether this was because of a dispute or simply because she did not apply for it.

Lieutenant Richard Groves
(Chichester House 1912–1915)

Died of wounds, Belgium, 24 October 1917 (aged 20)

Richard Groves was born in Salisbury, Rhodesia (now Harare, Zimbabwe) on 23 October 1897. He was the only son of Montague Groves, whose profession is unknown, and Ada Groves. While his parents continued to live in Rhodesia Groves was sent as a boarder first to Windlesham House School and then to the College, although they later settled in 10 Buckingham Road, Brighton.

Shortly after he left the College, Groves received a commission in the Nottinghamshire and Derbyshire Regiment (the Sherwood Foresters) and was attached to 6th Battalion, which formed part of 46th Division. However, he later transferred to the 11th Battalion Sherwood Foresters, which formed part of 23rd Division and it was

Left: Lieutenant Richard Groves (BCRH).

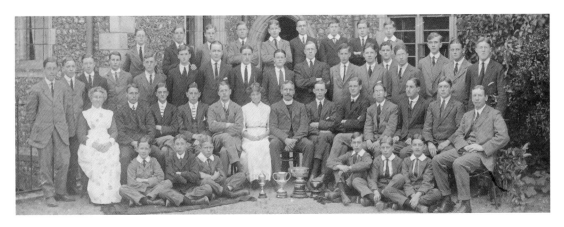

while serving with this unit at the Third Battle of Ypres (Passchendaele) that he sustained the wounds from which he was to die in a military hospital on 24 October 1917.

Groves's grave is in Wimereux Communal Cemetery, France. His grave, unusually, has a personalised inscription ordered by his parents, which reads: 'Beloved & only son of Montague & Ada Groves Rhodesia'.

2nd Lieutenant Charles William Homer (School House 1911–1912)

Accidentally killed while flying, Great Britain, 27 October 1917 (aged 23)

Charles Homer was born on 1 April 1894. His father's identity is unknown, possibly because he died before the 1901 Census, but he was the son of Mary Ann Homer (*née* Miller), who lived for some time in Bognor Regis and eventually settled in Euston, Suffolk. He was initially educated at Maidenhead College, Kent before moving to Brighton College (School House). During his brief period there he appears to have played in several football teams and was a member of the OTC. After he left the College he spent some months studying in Germany, before emigrating to New Zealand to take up sheep farming.

Homer was in New Zealand when the war began and initially enlisted with the NZEF, with which, as part of the ANZACs he fought at Gallipoli. After the evacuation from Gallipoli he transferred to the RFC, and after some training received both his aviation certificate and his commission. After serving on the Western Front for a period he became a flying instructor at Thetford Airfield, Norfolk. It was there that, on 27 October 1917, while flying with a pupil (Lt D. Gill) his plane had engine problems and crashed killing both him and his pupil.

Charles Homer was then buried in the churchyard of St Genevieve's Church, Euston, Suffolk.

Top: *Chichester House, 1914. Richard Groves is second row from the back, eighth boy from the right.*

Above: *2nd Lieutenant Charles William Homer (BCRH).*

Gunner Harold Dyson Wright (School House 1906–1908)

Killed in action, Belgium, 30 October 1917 (aged 27)

Harold Wright was born in Southport, Lancashire, on 16 November 1889. He was the youngest son and fourth child of Albert Wright, a shrimp merchant, and his wife Mary (*née* Dyson). There are few records of his time at the College. After leaving the College he followed his father into the shrimp business in Lancashire. However, his father's business was wound up in 1911 and it is unclear what he did from then until 1914. In 1911 he married Annie Eckerseley and in 1915 they had one daughter, Enid.

Following the outbreak of war he enlisted in the Royal Garrison Artillery and by 1917 was serving with the 405th Siege Battery RGA. He was killed in action on 30 October during the last days of the Third Battle of Ypres, when the Germans counter-attacked ferociously after the British had entered the village of Passchendaele.

Wright's grave is in Lijssenthoek Military Cemetery, Belgium.

Captain Henry Hall Griffith (Hampden House 1901–1909)

Accidentally killed while flying, Great Britain, 2 November 1917 (aged 26)

Henry Griffith was born in Brighton on 23 April 1891. He was the second son and third child of Arthur Griffith, a solicitor, and his wife Caroline (*née* Hall). After College he went up to Christ's College, Cambridge where he was an accomplished rower and a member of the engineering section of the OTC. After taking his degree he became an articled clerk in his father's firm but in the same year had an accident, which resulted in permanent injury to his knee.

On the outbreak of war Griffith was rejected by several branches of the armed services because of his damaged knee. However, in 1916 he received a commission in the RFC after learning to fly as a civilian at Hendon Flying School. He was to prove a successful and accomplished fighter pilot. On his second combat mission he shot down a German aircraft, forced another to land and then made a safe landing of his own despite damage to both his fuel tank and under-carriage. After nine months' service he returned home to England to act as an instructor at a training base in Dartford. While instructing trainees on 2 November 1917 he was killed in a flying accident.

Griffith is buried in the churchyard at St John the Evangelist, Newtimber, Hassocks, Sussex. His younger brother William Llewellyn Griffith OB was also killed in the war (see page 70).

Top: Harold Wright as a member of the Brighton College cricket team, 1906.

Above: Captain Henry Hall Griffith (BCRH).

Lieutenant Ewart Alan Mackintosh MC
(Junior House 1905–1909)

Killed in action, France, 21 November 1917 (aged 24)

FAREWELL

To Sergeant H. Fraser and L.-Sergeant G. M'Kay

WELL, you have gone now, comrades,
    And I shall see no more
The gallant friendly faces
Framed in my dug-out door.
I had no words to tell you
The things I longed to say,
But the company is empty
Since you have gone away.

The company is filled now
With faces strange to see,
And scarce a man of the old men
That lived and fought with me.
I know the drafts are good men,
I know they're doing well,
But they're not the men I slept with
Those nights at La Boiselle.

23

E. Alan Mackintosh.

Ewart Mackintosh was born on 4 March 1893 in Brighton. He was the younger son and fifth child of Alexander Mackintosh, a businessman, and his second wife Lillian (*née* Rogers). Alexander Mackintosh originated from Scotland and he had had a successful managerial and business career in both Britain and India before he became the Official Receiver in Sussex. While a pupil at the College Mackintosh won prizes for Greek and English and was a noted debater. In 1909 he won a scholarship to St Paul's School, London, where he published his

Above: *Ewart Mackintosh and a copy of his poem 'Farewell'.*

first poems in the school magazine, of which he was editor. In 1912 he went up to Christ Church, Oxford, to read Classics, where he took a second class in Mods in spring 1914 and joined the Oxford University OTC in the same year.

On the outbreak of war he immediately attempted to volunteer for service but was initially turned down due to his poor eyesight. However, he persisted and on 1 January 1915 he received a temporary commission in the Seaforth Highlanders. In July 1915 he was attached to the 5th Battalion Seaforths, which formed part of 51st Highland Division in France. In September 1915 he was promoted to Lieutenant and became the 'Bombing Officer' for the battalion, i.e. in command of supplying and organising raids in order to throw grenades at the enemy trenches. It was on such a raid in the Vimy Ridge area in May 1916 that he won the Military Cross for fulfilling a promise to his men not to abandon them. In the words of a letter he wrote to a friend:

> ... three of my men had their legs blown off and we had to pull them out ... I can tell you it was no joke pulling a helpless man a yard and then throwing a bomb to keep the Bosches back ... I promised the men I wouldn't leave the Bosche trench while there was a man alive in it and I kept my word ... All the men I brought back have [since] died.
>
> I believe I have been recommended for the Military Cross but I'd rather have the boys' lives ... I've had my taste of the show. It's not romantic. It's hell.

Throughout this period he wrote increasing numbers of poems, some of which were published as a collection called *A Highland Regiment* in January 1917.

During the Battle of the Somme, on 27 July 1916 Mackintosh was wounded in the knee and while wounded was further wounded in the eye by gas in the vicinity of High Wood. As a result he was invalided home and after making a partial recovery he was sent on an officers' course at Cambridge University prior to being posted to a training battalion. In October 1917 he returned to France, where he was attached to the 4th Seaforths, with whom he took part in the attack on Flesquières on the second day of the Battle of Cambrai. It was there that on 21 November 1917, while spotting for a Lewis gun, Mackintosh raised his head and was shot in the mouth and killed instantly.

Mackintosh's grave is in the Orival Wood Cemetery, Cambrai, France and an extract from one of his poems is reproduced on the Scottish–American War Memorial, Edinburgh. Two volumes of his poems were published: *A Highland Regiment and Other Poems* (1917) and *War, The Liberator, and Other Pieces* (1918). There is also a recent biography of Mackintosh by Colin Campbell and Rosalind Green: *Can't shoot a man with a cold: Lt. E. Alan Mackintosh MC 1893–1917 Poet of the Highland Division.*

2nd Lieutenant Leonard Bernard Lee (School House 1910–1915)

Killed in action, France, 30 November 1917 (aged 19)

Leonard Lee was born on 20 July 1898 in Streatham, London. He was the elder son of William Lee, a stockbroker, and his wife Florence (*née* Keeble). The family later moved from London to Brighton, where Lee attended the College. While a pupil Lee played in the cricket 1st XI and was a Sergeant in the OTC.

Opposite top: *Leonard Lee as a member of the Brighton College cricket team, 1915.*

After leaving the College in summer 1915, Lee immediately volunteered for service in the Royal Engineers and, after undergoing officer training, received his commission on 18 February 1916 and was attached to 83rd Field Company, Royal Engineers, which formed part of 20th Light Division. Lee fought with 20th Division on the Somme in 1916 and then in the advance on the Hindenburg Line in early 1917. Although the division did not take part in the Third Battle of Ypres (Passchendaele) it did take part in the Battle of Cambrai in late November 1917, in which a massed British tank attack broke the German lines. The Germans responded with a successful counter-attack, which experimented not with new weapons, like the British, but with new tactics, which proved almost as successful. It was during the German riposte that on 30 November 1917 Lee was killed in action as the German attacks penetrated right through the British lines to the support troops, such as the engineers, behind the third line of trenches.

Lee's grave is in the Flesquières Hill Cemetery, Cambrai, France.

Lieutenant George Henderson Tolson (School House 1903–1904)

Died of wounds, Palestine, 1 December 1917 (aged 28)

George Tolson was born on 24 July 1889 in Kensington, London. He was the only son and second child of George Tolson, a businessman, and his wife Anna (*née* Henderson). It appears that the family moved to Hove in the early 1900s, when Tolson was briefly a pupil at the College, although his sister Violet remained at a school in London. Tolson's career immediately after leaving the College is unclear. It is known, however, that in 1913 he emigrated to Canada, as his name appears on a disembarkation list for Montreal that year and he was resident in Canada when war broke out the following year.

Unsurprisingly, therefore, he initially volunteered for service with the CEF, with which he had reached the rank of Sergeant by September 1915, when he transferred to the London Regiment and received a commission as a 2nd Lieutenant. Following his commission Tolson was attached to the 18th Battalion, London Regiment (London Irish) – although he had no obvious Irish connections – which formed part of 60th Division. After a brief period in France in summer 1916 the division was sent to Salonika in November 1916 and then to Egypt and Palestine in July 1917. In late November 1917 Tolson's unit was involved in the early stages of the Jerusalem Campaign and he was seriously wounded in the course of the desperate Ottoman counter-attacks that took place from 28 November 1917 onwards. On 1 December 1917 he died of his wounds in a field hospital in the Jerusalem area.

Tolson's grave is in the Jerusalem War Cemetery, Israel.

Above: *Lieutenant George Henderson Tolson (BCRH).*

Major Raymond Douglas Belcher MC DSO
(School House 1892–1900)

Died of wounds, France, 7 December 1917 (aged 34)

Raymond Douglas Belcher was born on 5 March 1883 in Brighton. He was the youngest child (of seven children, including four sons) of Reverend Thomas Belcher, Head Master of the College between 1881 and 1893, and his wife Annie (née Neame). While at the College Belcher was a keen cricketer who played for the 1st XI in his final year and a successful athlete. He was less obviously academic than some in his family, although he does appear to have achieved the remarkable feat of winning a French prize despite being in set four of five. After leaving the College, Belcher obtained an engineering apprenticeship in Newcastle and began his career as an engineer and businessman. In 1906 his career took him to the Sudan where he worked for the 'Steamers and Navigation Department' on the Nile. After briefly returning to London in 1909 he then travelled to Argentina, then the boom economy of the World, where he worked for the Entre Ríos railway. Having completed his work for the railway it appears that he may have purchased an *estancia* (i.e. a large private estate) in the Corrientes region. However it is clear from his declaration in the Steam Ship *Demerara*'s manifest that his 'intended country of permanent residence' was Argentina.

Shortly after the outbreak of war Belcher returned to Britain solely, therefore, with the purpose of volunteering for service. In February 1915 he received a commission in the Royal Field Artillery and was attached to the 63rd Artillery Brigade (part of 12th Division), with whom he went to France in May 1915. For the next two and half years Belcher saw continuous fighting and was promoted first to Captain in 1916 and then to Major in 1917. He was wounded four times, mentioned in despatches twice and was awarded the MC in summer 1917 after he rallied a group of infantry who had fled the trench where he was posted as observer. On 30 November 1917 his battery was in action at Cambrai, where it was confronted by attacking waves of the infamous German storm troopers – they had broken through the main British lines to attack the artillery behind. In the course of this action Belcher was mortally wounded, but after his incapacitation one of his subordinates, Lieutenant Wallace, was able to repel the German attack for which he won the VC. Belcher died of his wounds seven days later at the Red Cross Hospital at Le Tréport.

Raymond Belcher is buried in the Mont Houn Military Cemetery, Le Tréport, France. A stained-glass window in the chapel in the school commemorates the lives and sacrifice of Belcher and his two brothers, Gordon Belcher OB and Harold Belcher OB (see page 113). His paternal first cousin Basil Belcher OB and his maternal first cousins Gerald Tassel-Neame OB and Geoffrey Neame OB were all also killed in the war. His other brother, Arthur Belcher OB, was Head Master of the College between 1933 and 1937.

Above: *Major Raymond Douglas Belcher MC DSO (BCRH).*

Lieutenant Robert George Bosworth Harvey
(School House 1906–1910)

Killed in action, France, 25 December 1917 (aged 22)

George Harvey was born on 5 September 1895 in Grantham, Lincolnshire. He was the only son and second child of George Harvey, a farmer, and his wife Emma (*née* Bosworth). There are few records of his time at the College save that he later completed his education at Grantham Grammar School.

Shortly after the outbreak of war Harvey enlisted in the 28th Battalion, London Regiment (Artists' Rifles) but after 18 months' service with the Artists' Rifles he received a commission in the Lincolnshire Regiment on 4 June 1916, in which he was attached to the 5th Battalion, which formed part of 46th Division. He served on the Western Front with the 5th Lincolnshires until his death, due to the premature detonation of a grenade on Christmas Day 1917. A fellow officer wrote to his father following his death that:

He was … absolutely fearless; would go anywhere, and was never happy unless he was worrying the enemy. He went over on a raid with me in September, and I cannot speak too highly of his conduct that night. We shall all miss his cheery presence among us …

Harvey's grave is in Cambrin Military Cemetery, Béthune, France.

Above: *Lieutenant Robert George Bosworth Harvey (BCRH).*

1918

German prisoners captured at the Battle of Amiens, 8 August 1918.

Private Lionel Frederick Vincent Hobson
(Junior and Chichester Houses 1894–1899)

Killed in action, Belgium, 19 March 1918 (aged 35)

Lionel Hobson was born in London on 28 February 1883. He was the younger son and second child of Frederick Hobson, a successful actor and comedian, and his wife Louisa (*née* Agate). Before he reached the age of ten both his parents had died and he lived with his uncle, Thomas Henry Hobson, in Brighton. While at the College he was in the football and cricket 2nd XI, being described as 'a good fielder but a timid bat', and played the triangle in a school concert. After leaving the College he inherited a large sum left in trust for him by his father, which enabled him to live 'on his own means' and to marry Agnes Wright in 1909. In 1911 the couple lived in Balham, Surrey (now London) and had two children, Lionel (1909–1990) and Dorothy (1912–2003).

On the outbreak of war Hobson initially enlisted in the Royal Field Artillery but over the course of the war he was transferred to a number of different units – the 15th Battalion, King's Liverpool Regiment, the 3rd Battalion Border Regiment and finally the 11th Battalion, Border Regiment (the Lonsdale Pals), which formed part of 32nd Division. It was with this unit that on 19 March 1918 he was killed in action in Flanders.

Hobson's grave is in the Artillery Wood Cemetery, Ypres, Belgium.

Major Roger Frederick Curtis King
(School House 1892)

Died, Great Britain, 19 March 1918 (aged 43)

Roger King was born on 19 December 1874 in Chatham, Kent. He was the only son and second child of Lieutenant-Colonel Frederick King (Middlesex Regiment), a retired army officer and brewer, and his wife Jane (*née* Durant). While King was a child the family moved to Walburton near Arundel, Sussex. As a pupil at the College he played a total of eleven matches for the 1st and 2nd XI football teams. He played at half-back and left wing and is recorded in the report of one match against Lancing for his 'resolute play and clever heading'. After leaving the College he, like his father, received a commission in the Middlesex Regiment and was promoted to the rank of Captain during the Boer War before leaving the army in 1911 to become an insurance broker in London. Shortly thereafter his mother was widowed and he moved with her to a farm near Lewes.

Above: *Private Lionel Frederick Vincent Hobson (BCRH).*

Following the outbreak of war he re-joined the army and was attached to the 6th Battalion, Middlesex Regiment, a home service battalion used for duties such as guarding Chatham Docks, then a major naval base. In 1917 he fell ill and was sent to a Voluntary Aid Detachment hospital in Uxbridge, Middlesex, where he died on 19 March 1918. The cause of his death is unclear but his lengthy stay in hospital indicates that he must have been seriously ill for some time.

King's grave is in the churchyard at St Peter's, Hamsey, near Lewes alongside that of his mother, who had died in June 1915.

Lieutenant Eric Williams
(Hampden House 1909–1910)

Killed in action, France, 27 March 1918 (aged 23)

Eric Williams was born in June 1894 in Bradford, Yorkshire. He was the only son and second child of Thomas Williams, a Congregationalist pastor, and his wife Ellen (née Henry). Thomas Williams had initially been a coal miner in Wales before training to be a Congregationalist minister and ministering first to Greenfield Church, Bradford (1888–1909) and then to Queen Square Church, Brighton (1909–1931). Eric was therefore educated in Bradford until he attended the College for one year. There are few records of his time as a pupil save that he left to become a bank clerk.

Following the outbreak of war he received a commission in the West Yorkshire Regiment and in 1915 he was attached to the 2nd Bradford Pals (18th Battalion, West Yorkshire Regiment), which indicates that his connection with Yorkshire was still very strong. He briefly served with the battalion on the Suez Canal, and then, in March 1916, accompanied it to the Somme area of the Western Front, where it formed part of 31st Division. In the context of the BEF's manpower crisis in winter 1917/18, which was in part caused by Lloyd George's refusal to release reserves from the United Kingdom, the 2nd Bradford Pals were disbanded and Williams was transferred to 2nd Battalion, West Yorkshire Regiment. The 2nd West Yorkshires, which formed part of 8th Division, were in the ill-fated British Fifth Army and, as such, bore the brunt of what has become known as the 'Ludendorff offensive' from 21 March 1918 onwards. On 27 March 1918 Williams was killed in action during the Battle of Rosières, one of the small actions in which the British attempted to stall the Ludendorff offensive.

Williams has no known grave but he is commemorated on the Pozières Memorial, Pozières, France.

Above: *Lieutenant Eric Williams (BCRH).*

Major Geoffrey Neame MC (Junior House 1893–1897)

Killed in action, France, 2 April 1918 (aged 34)

Geoffrey Neame was born on 8 January 1884 in Faversham, Kent. He was the eldest son and first child, among six, of Frederick Neame, a land agent and farmer from the Neame brewing family, and his wife Kathleen (née Stunt). After leaving Brighton Neame went to Cheltenham College and thereafter joined his father as a farmer in Kent.

Shortly after the outbreak of war he received a commission in the Royal Field Artillery and was attached to the 190th Brigade RFA, which formed part of 41st Division (one of the later 'New Army' divisions that moved to France in May 1916). While serving with the 190th Brigade RFA he was awarded the Military Cross in March 1918, for his actions some months earlier when he personally put out a fire in an ammunition pit which had been caused by enemy shelling. On 2 April Neame was killed in action by enemy shellfire near Bucquoy in Artois, while his unit was in the successful British attempt to repulse the Ludendorff offensive.

Neame's grave is in Bienvillers Military Cemetery, Arras, France. Four of Neame's first cousins, Gerald Tassel-Neame OB, Raymond Belcher OB, Gordon Belcher OB, and Harold Belcher OB, were also killed in the war.

George Stanley King (Hampden House 1908–1911)

Died of wounds, France, 30 April 1918 (aged 22)

Private George Stanley King was born in Grantham, Lincolnshire, on 7 September 1895. He was the son of Edward King, a commercial traveller, and his wife Eleanor, whom Edward King had married in New York. Details about King's time at the College are unclear, although he was certainly not the only Old Brightonian of the period to originate from Lincolnshire.

After leaving the College King must have emigrated to Canada, where his parents may have had connections, because, rather than joining one of the English County Regiments, he enlisted in the 7th Battalion, British Columbian Regiment, which formed part of 1st Canadian Division. As such he was a member of one of the elite divisions of the BEF, one that was to fight with distinction on the infamous Vimy Ridge in April 1917 and then to be thrown in as a last resort into the desperate battles fought to stem the Ludendorff offensives in spring 1918. King died of wounds on 30 April 1918 following injuries sustained in the Arras area during the last stage of the Ludendorff offensive.

King's grave is in the Commonwealth War Cemetery at Ligny-St Flochel, Averdoingt, France.

Top: *Major Geoffrey Neame MC (BCRH).*

Above: *George Stanley King (BCRH).*

Sub-Lieutenant Egbert Wilfrid Leslie Ravenhill Hulbert (Durnford House 1912–1914)

Killed in action, France, 25 May 1918 (aged 19)

Egbert Hulbert was born on 6 December 1898 in Steyning, Sussex. He was the youngest son and fourth child of Major Harry Hulbert, an estate agent in Brighton, and his wife May (*née* Soper). Details of Hulbert's period at the College or his immediate career on leaving the school are unclear as he appears both to have enlisted in the HAC and been a member of the RNVR in 1916.

However, by early 1918 he had received a commission in the Navy and from 20 April 1918 was attached to the Hood Battalion, which formed part of the (63rd) Royal Naval Division. The Hood Battalion, like most of the other units in 63rd Division, was composed of naval personnel fighting as infantry on the Western Front. On 25 May 1918 he was killed by enemy shellfire in the Somme area.

Hulbert's grave is in the Mesnil Communal Cemetery, Mesnil, France.

Top: *Sub-Lieutenant Egbert Wilfred Leslie Ravenhill Hulbert (BCRH).*

Above: *Egbert Leslie Hulbert Cup, presented to Brighton College by his parents as 'a memorial of his happy days while at Brighton College, and of his glorious death in The Great War on May 25th 1918.'*

Lieutenant Francis Wilfrid Butt
(Hampden House 1914–1915)

Killed in action, France, 26 May 1918 (aged 18)

Francis Butt was born in Gloucester on 8 June 1899. He was the elder son and first child of Reverend Arthur Butt, Rector of Rodmorton, Gloucestershire, and his wife Dora (née Nolan). The family subsequently moved to Brighton and as a consequence Butt was briefly a pupil at the College. It is unclear what Butt did immediately after leaving the school but it is possible that he may have intended to join the legal profession because he enlisted immediately in the Inns of Court OTC.

Sometime thereafter he trained as a pilot and received a commission in the RFC, which was combined with the RNAS to form the RAF on 1 April 1918. Butt was attached to the 102nd Squadron RAF, a specialist unit formed in August 1917 to conduct night-time bombing raids using FE2b biplanes. The science of night flying was still in its infancy and the operations of the 102nd Squadron were therefore extremely dangerous. After initial training the unit was moved to France in the spring of 1918, where it conducted bombing raids on the railways in occupied Northern France and Belgium that the Germans used for their supplies. It was on one such mission that Butt was killed in action on 26 May 1918.

Butt's body was recovered and his grave is now in Doullens Communal Cemetery, Doullens, France.

2nd Lieutenant William Humphrey Cole Cornish Silver
(Hampden House 1895–1896)

Killed in action, France, 8 June 1918 (aged 36)

William Silver was born in September 1883 in Chislehurst, Kent. He was the third child and younger son of Colonel Hugh Adams Silver, a retired army officer and successful businessman, with his second wife Anne Cornish (née Daniels). Silver had a further twelve elder half-siblings by his father's first marriage to Annie Ellen Daniels (who died in 1876). Silver's father was the heir to the Silver Clothing Company, which gave its name to Silvertown in London's Docklands.

It appears that Silver spent some of the nineteen years between leaving the College and the outbreak of the First World

Top: *Lieutenant Francis Wilfrid Butt (BCRH).*

Left: *2nd Lieutenant William Humphrey Cole Cornish Silver (BCRH).*

War as a poultry farmer in Kent but his exact circumstances are unclear. On the outbreak of war Silver enlisted in the Queen's Own 1st West Kent Yeomanry, a territorial cavalry regiment. The West Kent Yeomanry saw extensive service in the eastern Mediterranean, both at Gallipoli and in the defence of the Suez Canal, and in February 1917 was converted into an infantry battalion as the 10th Battalion, East Kent Regiment (the 'Buffs'), in the course of which Silver was promoted to Corporal. Shortly thereafter Silver trained as an officer and in December 1917 received a commission in the Sussex Regiment. In April 1918 he was attached to the 2nd Battalion, Sussex Regiment, which formed part of 1st Division on the Western Front. On 8 June 1918, Silver was killed while his new unit was engaged in a trench raid in the Noeux-les-Mines area.

Following his death his commanding officer wrote to his mother:

> Although your son had only been with us a short time he was universally popular in a quiet way, and everyone is very sad at his going. Personally I have lost a good friend ... Your son was the coolest man under fire that I have ever seen ... On one occasion, after fourteen hours continuous trench duty he voluntarily did another five to relieve another officer who was not well. Although he was about six years my senior he took orders from me without question or comment, and, altogether one could not wish for a better officer.

Silver's grave is in Cambrin Military Cemetery, Pas de Calais, France.

Private Roy Hammersley Field
(Durnford 1913–1916)

Died of wounds, France, 29 June 1918 (aged 19)

Roy Field was born on 8 February 1899 in Leytonstone, Essex. He was the youngest son and fourth child of Alfred Field, who owned a stationery business, and his wife Agnes (*née* Latilla). By 1911 the family were living in Purley, Surrey. While at the College Field was in the football 1st and 2nd XIs.

After leaving the school Field enlisted in the 28th Battalion London Regiment, commonly known as the Artists' Rifles, which formed part of 63rd Division, which was normally known as the 'Royal Naval Division' because the majority of its units, with the exception of Field's battalion, were members of the Royal Navy. In mid-1918 63rd Division, after facing Ludendorff's second spring offensive in Flanders, was sent to the Somme, which was then, albeit briefly, a quiet part of the front. Nonetheless in late June 1918 Field was wounded and, as a result, died in hospital on 29 June 1918.

Field's grave is in the Bagneux British Cemetery, Gazaincourt, France.

Above: *Roy Field in the Brighton College football team, 1915.*

Lieutenant Robert Edmund Horton
(Junior and School Houses 1909–1916)

Died of wounds, France, 13 August 1918 (aged 20)

Robert Edmund Horton was born in France on 4 November 1897. He was one of two children of Charles Horton and his wife Edith (*née* Salmon). There is very little trace of the family in the public records and it may be that the family lived in France throughout Horton's childhood. The one record that does survive is, very unusually for the period, a petition for divorce on grounds of adultery filed by Horton's mother Edith in 1914 against her husband. While a pupil at the College Horton played for the cricket 2nd XI as well as being a school prefect and serving as a Lance-Corporal in the OTC. After leaving the College, Horton received a commission in the RFC. In 1918 he was attached to the 243rd Squadron RAF, based in Cherbourg, where he acted as an observer in Wight seaplanes being flown for maritime observation over the Channel. On 13 August 1918 he was killed instantly in an air accident in which his pilot, Lieutenant Mossop, also sustained fatal injuries.
Horton's grave is in Tourlaville Communal Cemetery, Manche, France.

Captain Victor Arnold Bone (Durnford 1912–1914)

Killed in action, Macedonia, 18 September 1918 (aged 21)

Victor Bone was born in Llandudno, Wales, on 7 February 1897. He was the third son and sixth child of Ernst Bone, a solicitor, and his wife Bessie (*née* Evans). On 22 September 1914 he received a commission in the Welsh Fusiliers and in October was attached to the 11th Battalion, Welsh Fusiliers, a 'New Army' unit then being formed in Wrexham.
In September 1915 the battalion, which formed part of 22nd Division, was sent to France but shortly thereafter was sent to Salonika where it was to remain for the rest of the war. For much of the war the Macedonian theatre was quiet, but on 16 September 1918 an offensive was launched in order to liberate Serbia and drive Germany's Bulgarian allies out of the war. On 18 September, Bone, now promoted to Captain, was killed in action during an assault on the Bulgarian fortifications at Doiran in which, despite extensive use of airpower to attack the Bulgarian positions, the Bulgarians were able to pick off the attacking troops one by one.
Bone's grave is in the Doiran Military Cemetery, Salonika, Greece.

Top: *Lieutenant Robert Edmund Horton (BCRH).*

Above: *Captain Victor Arnold Bone (BCRH).*

2nd Lieutenant Richard Norton
(School House 1911–1916)

Killed in action, France, 18 September 1918 (aged 19)

Richard Norton was born on 14 March 1899 in Mayfair, London. He was the only child of Dr Richard Norton, a successful doctor, and his wife Mabel (*née* Hooper). There are few records of his time at the College, although there is some evidence that he spent much of his holidays with the Hall family in Marcham, Berkshire, rather than at home with his parents.

Shortly after leaving the College, Norton began officer training and on 20 December 1917 he received a commission in the Norfolk Regiment. He was then attached to the 9th Battalion, which formed part of 24th Division. During 1918 he fought in many of the key actions that took place following the Ludendorff offensive. Later in the year 24th Division was involved in the attack on Épehy, which was a successful attempt to take a series of German outposts before the main assault on the Hindenburg Line. In the course of the attack Norton was killed in action on 18 September 1918.

Norton's grave is in the Chappelle British Cemetery, Holnon, France.

Sergeant Major William Edward Price
(School House 1906)

Killed in action, Palestine, 21 September 1918 (aged 28)

William Edward Price was born in Slimbridge, Gloucestershire on 19 February 1890. He was the eldest son and second child of John Price, a farmer, and his wife Rebecca. It is unclear why Price spent a short period as a pupil at the College aged 16 and there is little record of his achievements while he was there. After he left the College, Price worked with his father on his farm in Gloucestershire.

On the outbreak of war Price enlisted in the Gloucestershire Hussars, a regiment of Yeomanry cavalry that formed part of the Yeomanry Division. He first saw action, as a private, in the Egyptian theatre in April 1915. Over the course of the war Price was promoted through the non-commissioned ranks, reaching the rank of Sergeant Major in 1918. The Gloucestershire Hussars, unlike the other Yeomanry regiments, were not sent to France in 1918

Top: *2nd Lieutenant Richard Norton (BCRH).*

Above: *Sergeant Major William Edward Price (BCRH).*

but instead remained in Palestine as part of 5th Cavalry Division. Price was killed in action near Nazareth on 21 September 1918 during the fast-moving and victorious 'Battle of Armageddon' (or Meddigo), which involved some of the last successful cavalry charges in history and resulted in the final destruction of the Ottoman Army.

Price's grave is in the Haifa War Cemetery, Israel.

Captain Alfred Herbert Westwood (School House 1905–1909)

Killed in action, France, 21 September 1918 (aged 28)

Alfred Westwood was born on 4 August 1890 in Handsworth, Birmingham. He was the younger son of William Westwood, a 'refiner and bullion dealer', and his wife Elizabeth (*née* Barnett). Westwood had a successful academic and sporting career at the College. He played for 1st XI and 2nd XI football teams, although one match report noted, 'he goes very hard, but has little control over the ball.' He was also a Colour Sergeant in the OTC, a school prefect and a member of the so-called 'Play-ground' committee, which appears to have been set up to oversee extra-curricular activities. In 1910 he went up to Christ's College, Cambridge, where he rowed for his College and, according to the 'Cambridge Letter' sent by Old Brightonian undergraduates to the school magazine, may have been involved in some kind of motorcycle accident:

We know that P Hazeldine [another OB] has been guilty of gross cruelty to a motor bike, and that Westwood was present throughout the whole journey, but did not once intervene.

He left Cambridge in 1912 without taking his degree, and his career between then and summer 1914 is unknown.

On 14 September 1914, shortly after the outbreak of war, he received a commission in the Royal Warwickshire Regiment. He was attached to the 10th Battalion Warwickshire Regiment, which, after a period of training, was sent to the Western Front in July 1915. Westwood was wounded in August 1915 and then again in August 1916 before being promoted to Captain and transferred to the 6th Battalion Northamptonshire Regiment in 1918. On 21 September 1918 he was killed in action near Cambrai on the Western Front during the successful attempt to breach the Hindenburg Line.

Westwood's grave is in Perrone Communal Cemetery Extension, Perrone, France.

Above: *Captain Alfred Herbert Westwood (BCRH).*

Opposite top: *2nd Lieutenant Cyril Frederick Ernest West (BCRH).*

Opposite bottom: *Geoffrey Alwyn Bonser (BCRM).*

2nd Lieutenant Cyril Frederick Ernest West
(Durnford House 1912–1916)

Killed in action, Belgium, 28 September 1918 (aged 19)

Cyril West was born on 21 December 1898 in Wandsworth, London. He was the only son and second child of George West, a railway contractor and subsequently manager of a Steel Mill, and his wife Lucretia (*née* Hollingsworth). The family subsequently moved to West Byfleet, Surrey. While at the College, West was a member of the cricket and football 2nd XI and a Sergeant in the OTC.

After leaving the College, West went to RMC Sandhurst for officer training and in May 1918 received a commission in the Royal Sussex Regiment. During summer 1918 he was attached to the 6th Battalion, Wiltshire Regiment, which formed part of 14th Division. He was then killed in action on 28 September 1918 during the final battles of the war in Flanders, known as the 'Fifth Battle of Ypres'. Unusually, one of his subordinates, a Sergeant in his platoon, wrote to his father following his death to say that:

Your son died like the hero he was: like an officer and a gentleman. He had no fear of death: a braver lad never made the supreme sacrifice.

West's grave is in Perth Cemetery (China Wall), Ypres, Belgium.

Captain Geoffrey Alwyn Bonser
(Hampden House 1898–1902)

Killed in action, Belgium, 29 September 1918 (aged 29)

Geoffrey Bonser was born on 3 February 1889 in Ashfield, Nottinghamshire. He was the only son and second child of Geoffrey Bonser, who held various posts in local government such as Chairman of the School Board, and his wife Dorothy (*née* Sims). It is unclear why the family came to Brighton from the Midlands and then returned again as Geoffrey Bonser held similar local government posts in both localities. After four years at the College Bonser gained an honorary scholarship to King's School Worcester and then went up to St John's College, Cambridge, graduating in Natural Sciences in 1910. He then went on to St Thomas's Hospital, London, where he qualified as a surgeon in 1914.

Shortly after the outbreak of war he enlisted in the RAMC and was initially posted to the Eastern General Military Hospital, Cambridge, where he received his commission on 15 July 1915.

On 23 April 1916 he was promoted to Captain and attached, as Medical Officer, to the 12th Battalion, Norfolk Regiment, which formed part of 74th Division. In 1917 he was posted to Palestine from where he wrote home about the stress of treating the wounded following the Battle of Beersheba, the lack of sleep and the discomfort caused by the cold nights and baking hot days. However, he also wrote about visiting various sites mentioned in the Bible, such as 'the Valley of Aujon where, you will remember, Joshua made the moon stand still' and, more contemporaneously, the 'Jew's [sic] wailing place' in Jerusalem. In summer 1918 he returned home on leave, where he married Lilian Prime on 3 July 1918. In late summer 1918 he was sent to Belgium, again with the 12th Battalion, Norfolk Regiment. It was there that on 29 September 1918 he was killed, in the words of his Colonel:

> ... instantaneously by a shell while attending the wounded ... He is a great loss to the battalion and from all those around him I have heard nothing but praise.

Bonser's grave is in Strand Military Cemetery, Belgium.

2nd Lieutenant Frederic Leslie Hedgcock (School House 1913–1917)

Killed in action, France, 29 September 1918 (aged 20)

Frederic Hedgcock (known as 'Leslie') was born in Reading on 7 August 1898. He was the youngest son and third child of Edwin Hedgcock, who ran a successful drapery business, and his wife Clarinda. While at the College he was a Lance Corporal in the OTC. The commander of the Brighton College OTC reported in his recommendation to the army that he was 'always keen on his work in the OTC' and was expected 'to make a useful and painstaking officer'.

After leaving the College in spring 1917 Hedgcock initially joined the Berkshire Regiment but later received a commission in the Machine Gun Corps in October 1917. He was then attached to the 57th Battalion, Machine Gun Corps, and was killed in action on 29 September 1918 during the final victorious campaign of the war.

Hedgcock's grave is in the Commonwealth War Cemetery in Anneux, France.

Above: *2nd Lieutenant Frederic Leslie Hedgcock (BCRH).*

Opposite top: *2nd Lieutenant Colin Keith Dufferin (Mackenzie) Campbell (BCRH).*

Opposite bottom: *2nd Lieutenant Charles Herbert Burt (BCRH).*

2nd Lieutenant Colin Keith Dufferin (Mackenzie) Campbell (Hampden House 1910–1912)

Died of wounds, France, 30 September 1918 (aged 21)

Colin Campbell (also known as Mackenzie) was born on 13 September 1897 in Calcutta, India. He was the son of Leslie S. Campbell, Personal Assistant to Chief of Staff, India, and his wife Mary. There are few records of Campbell's time at the College or his career thereafter. However, it seems likely that between 1912 and 1914 he emigrated to Australia because he joined the Australian forces during the war.

He received a commission in the 58th Australian Battalion, AIF, which in 1918 formed part of 15th Brigade, 5th Australian Division. Campbell died of wounds sustained in the Battle of St Quentin, an engagement during the final offensive of the war, on 30 September 1918.

Campbell's grave is in the Tincourt New British Cemetery, Peronne, France.

2nd Lieutenant Charles Herbert Burt (Junior House 1895–1899)

Died, Ireland, 27 October 1918 (aged 32)

Charles Burt was born on 6 October 1886 in Marylebone, London. He was the younger son and fifth child of Henry W. Burt, a solicitor, and his wife Fanny. Burt's family lived in London throughout his life, his sisters remaining there after both his parents apparently died while he was still a child. However, he was sent to the College aged 9 and then went to Fettes College. After completing his education he became a clerk in a shipping firm in London.

On the outbreak of war he joined the County of London Yeomanry, a Territorial Cavalry Regiment. He was attached to the 3rd Battalion, which, apart from one detachment which served in the Middle East, was converted into a cyclist battalion and retained in the United Kingdom throughout the war. In October 1918 he contracted an illness, probably a variant of the Spanish flu then sweeping Europe, while stationed at Curragh, Ireland, and was hospitalised in Dublin, where he died on 27 October 1918.

Burt's body was repatriated to England and his grave is in the Dorking Cemetery, Surrey.

Lieutenant Keith Macdonald Scobie
(Hampden House 1910–1914)

Accidentally killed, Great Britain, 27 October 1918 (aged 21)

Keith Scobie was born in Scotland on 1 January 1897. He was the younger son of Donald Scobie, an engineer with the Indian Public Works Department, and his wife Joan (*née* McEwen). Unlike his elder brother, Scobie was not born in India but the family returned there shortly afterwards and continued to live there until his mother's death in 1900. After the family's return to Britain Scobie first attended Wadham House Preparatory School before progressing to the College, where he was a leading light in the debating society and an enthusiast for 'modern literature'. He was also, unsurprisingly, in the OTC, although he remained a private.

After leaving the College Keith Scobie appears to have spent a year preparing for the army entrance examination, which he passed in September 1915 (being placed 35th) and entered the RMA Woolwich. This was a relatively unusual route into the army during wartime but it appears that he took the decision to train to be a specialist officer in a technical branch rather than commissioning straight into an infantry regiment after a relatively short period of training like most of his peers. In May 1916 he received a commission in the RGA and was subsequently attached to the 140th Siege Battery during the Battle of the Somme. On 2 April 1917, while on secondment to the ANZACs, he was injured by a high explosive shell at Bapaume, after which he was invalided back to Britain and sent to Somerville Hospital in Oxford. It appears that although the initial wound was superficial he was afflicted with other health problems and did not return to duty until October 1917, when he became an instructor at the Aldershot Siege School. During the intervening period, when Scobie was invalided, his commanding officer attempted to recommend him for a number of gallantry awards but Scobie himself declined these on the basis that 'he had done nothing worthy of special notice'. In April 1918, following the creation of the RAF, Scobie volunteered for pilot training at the 43rd Training Station, Chattis Hill, Hampshire. It was there that, having received his pilot's licence, he was killed in a flying accident on 27 October 1918.

Scobie's grave is in the military cemetery at Andover, Hampshire. After his death, in accordance with his wishes, Scobie's father printed several copies of an anthology of poems entitled *A Sheaf of Poems* 'for private circulation and presentation to a few of his friends'. A copy of this collection, complete with a dedication to Keith Scobie by his father, is deposited at the British Library. His brother, John Scobie OB was also killed in the war (see page 82).

Top: *Lieutenant Keith Macdonald Scobie (BCRH).*

Above: *21 Rutland Gardens in Hove: one of the houses Keith and John Scobie lived in while attending Brighton College.*

Major General Nikolai Sergeivitch de Plaoutine (Fr.)/ Plautin (Ru.) (Principal's House 1884–1886)

Died of smallpox, Poland/Ukraine, around 31 October 1918 (aged 50)

Nikolai de Plaoutine was born in Nice, France on 2 February 1868. He was the eldest son of Serge Plautin, a member of the Russian gentry who was sometime aide-de-camp to Tsar Alexander II, and his English wife Eleanor (*née* Pringle). His family appear to have alternated freely between the Frenchified version of their name 'de Plaoutine' and the Russian version 'Plautin', a common fashion among upper-class Russian families during the nineteenth century. Shortly after his birth the family returned to Russia where they lived in Tsarskoe Selo, where most of de Plaoutine's younger siblings were born, and later St Petersburg. Nonetheless it is evident that, probably owing to his English mother, a strong connection with Britain remained, which accounts for the two years he spent at the College during the 1880s. On returning to Russia he embarked on a military career, becoming Colonel of the Tersko-Dagestansky Cavalry Regiment in around 1904 and married Maria Mikhailovna Raevskaya, a member of a very prominent Russian noble family who may have been a Lady in Waiting to the Dowager Tsarina Maria Feodorovna.

After the outbreak of war de Plaoutine was given command of the 2nd Brigade of Combined Cossack Division and later, it appears, promoted to Major General and given command of a division of Kuban Cossacks, although this may have been in the early stages of the Russian Civil War rather than in the First World War itself. College records state that he 'suffered horribly in the Revolution' and then died of the 'Black Pox', i.e. smallpox, somewhere in the western border areas (i.e. Poland and Ukraine) of the former Russian Empire in late autumn 1918. De Plaoutine's family were certainly persecuted and in some cases either exiled or executed during the Civil War which followed the Russian Revolution in 1917; for example, both

Above left: *Nikolai de Plaoutine with his family, c. 1888.*

Above right: *Nikolai de Plaoutine in his Cossack uniform, c. 1905.*

his brother and one of his sisters were executed in 1918 and 1921 respectively. However, the exact circumstances of his death, including whether or not it took place in captivity, are unknown, although the cause of death appears credible because the chaos that sprang from war and revolution did result in a smallpox epidemic in Ukraine.

The location of de Plaoutine's grave is unknown. His wife, like many other members of the Russian aristocracy, moved into exile in France, and died in Algiers, then part of Metropolitan France, in 1942.

2nd Lieutenant Herman Grant Oxley
(School House 1906–1910)

Killed in action, France, 4 November 1918 (aged 25)

Herman Grant Oxley was born on 19 July 1893 in Bexley Heath, Kent. He was the fifth son and youngest child of George Oxley, a schoolmaster, and his wife Alice (*née* Brown). When Herman Oxley was in his early teens it appears that the family moved from Bexley Heath to Hove. There are few records of Oxley's career at the College but it is clear that after he left aged 17 his family moved to Sunningdale, Berkshire, and he became a clerk at Coutts Bank in the Strand.

Shortly after the outbreak of war Oxley joined the Inns of Court OTC and in August 1915 received a commission in the King's Royal Rifle Corps (KRRC). He was then attached to 16th Battalion KRRC and on 15 July 1916 was severely wounded during fierce fighting at High Wood, which was part of the Somme campaign. He then spent some months in hospital and after being discharged was declared unfit for further military service. However in 1918, following what appears to have been a clerical error, he was, apparently willingly, readmitted into the army. After taking a Lewis Gun course at Woolwich he was sent to France in summer 1918 where he participated in the allied advance that autumn which ended in final victory. On 4 November 1918 Oxley was involved in an action near the Sambre Canal south of Catillon in which he and his men were pinned down on a river bank by enemy fire. Oxley was killed in action while trying to wade or swim across the river because he could not reach a bridge that was about a mile downstream.

Oxley's grave is in the Highland Cemetery, Le Cateau, France.

Top: *47 Marine Parade, Brighton, where de Plaoutine lived while attending College.*

Above: *Portrait photograph of Herman Oxley.*

Lieutenant Arthur Cave
(Hampden House 1909–1913)

Died of pneumonia, Great Britain, 10 November 1918 (aged 22)

Arthur Cave was born on 27 March 1896 in Colombo, Ceylon (now Sri Lanka). He was the elder son of Samuel Cave, a 'buyer of fancy goods' for the Ceylon Business House, and his wife Grace. Although Cave was born in Ceylon the family evidently moved back to Britain during his childhood and in 1909 he was sent to the College. While at the College, he played for the 1st XI football and cricket teams and was also Captain of Gym, as well as serving in the OTC. On leaving the College he returned to Ceylon to work in business, where he enlisted in the part-time Ceylon Planters' Rifle Corps.

However, after the outbreak of war he returned to Britain and in May 1915 entered RMC Sandhurst and received a commission in the Durham Light Infantry in September 1915, with whom he ultimately rose to Captain. In 1918 he transferred to the newly formed RAF and was undergoing pilot training at Marston when he became infected with influenza (part of the Spanish flu epidemic). He was transferred to the Military Hospital, Chatham, but died on 10 November 1918.

Cave's grave is in the Brighton City Cemetery, Sussex.

Unit	Regtl. No.	Name	Rank and Initials	Date of Death	Plot	Row	Grave	Type of Memorial	Type of Grave	Remarks Next-of-kin.
Roy: Fus:	17716	HOMES.	Pte: A.	16.7.19.	MA.		90.	NM	R.	Mrs. G.Sined. 38 London St. Brighton.
A. A. M. C.	32012	FUNNELL.	Cpl:J.G.E.	11.1.16.	KA.		33.			Mrs. Funnell. 6 Franklin Rd. Brighton.
Labour Corps.	135033	HAYLER.	Pte. W.J.	17.3.18.	PF.		58.			Mrs. Hayler. 25 Queens Gdns: N.Rd. B'on
Labour Corps) late R.G.A.)	571986) 753)	PARSONS.	Cpl:CGA.	6.1.20.	DA.		18.			Mrs. S.W.Parsons. 18. New England St. B'on.
R. E.	1842452	STEDMAN.	L/Cpl: J.	19.4.21.	ZIF		89			
R. F. A.	97836.	JESSON.	Sdlr: T.	24.3.15.	PT.		73			Mrs. M.J.Jesson. 9. Ashton St. Brighton.
23/T. R. Bn:	8074.	SHORT.	Cpl.F.W.	8.12.16.	BK		82			Mrs. E. Short. 79 Brading Rd. Brighton.
11/Sussex Rgt:	G/11539.	FEIST.	Pte. H.J.	8.9.17.	PF.		87.			Mr. L.A.Feist. 34 Viaduct Rd.Brighton.
L. N. Lancs:	3846819.	DAVIES.	Sgt: J.L.	10.7.21.	ZIF		86			
9/W. Riding Rgt:		AMESBURY.	Major F.G.D.	7.2.18.	NM		90			Mrs.F.G.D.Amesbury. 77 Quay Rd. Bridlington. Yorks.
R.Sussex Rgt:	315309.	FOORD.	Pte. A.	21.9.19.	A. 2.KA		1039.	NM		Mrs. E.L.Foord. 29 Whichels Place. B'on.
D.L.I. & R.A.F.		CAVE.	Lt. A.D.	10.11.18.	ZIX		72	P.P.		Mrs. S. Cave, 16 College Terrace. B'on.
R. A. F.		SHARMAN.	2/Lt. C.L.	22.2.19.	TP.		53			

Top: *Arthur Cave in the Brighton College football team, 1912.*

Above: *Graves Registration Form, which includes an entry for Arthur Cave.*

AFTERMATH

The Cemetery, Etaples, 1919.

Captain Gilbert Maurice Parkinson
(School House 1910–1913)

Died of pneumonia, Italy, 14 November 1918 (aged 22)

Gilbert Maurice Parkinson was born in Wandsworth in 1896. He was the younger son of William Parkinson OB, whose profession is unknown, and his wife Florence. Shortly after Parkinson's admission to the College he was awarded the German Prize. He also played as a right wing in the 1st XI football team and was Sergeant in the OTC. After leaving the College he commenced officer training at RMC Sandhurst in winter 1913.

Shortly after the outbreak of war, on 19 November 1914, he received a commission in the Northumberland Fusiliers and went to France to join the BEF, where he immediately saw action with the 1st Battalion Northumberland Fusiliers at the First Battle of Ypres. In May 1915 he was wounded and invalided back to England where he remained until December 1917, when he became an instructor at the Central Military School in France. He subsequently volunteered for service in Italy as part of the small British force which operated there in support of the Italians following their terrible defeat at Caporetto in November 1917. In July 1918 he was promoted to Captain and became the British liaison officer to the Italian 33rd Division. Unfortunately he was then struck down in the influenza epidemic that ravaged Europe in the closing months of the war and died in Bordighera, Italy on 14 November 1918, just after the end of the war.

Parkinson's grave is in the Bordighera British Cemetery, San Remo, Italy and he is commemorated on a memorial in Brighton College Chapel (see picture on contents page). Both are inscribed with the words taken from Dante: *E'n la sua volontade e nostra pace* (in His will is our peace). An impressive portrait of Gilbert and his brother William by Maurice Goldhagen can be found in the Northumberland Fusiliers Museum.

Captain Walter Reginald Grant (Bazett's House 1890–1891)

Died in Great Britain, 26 November 1918 (aged 42)

Walter Grant was born on 6 May 1876 in Lambeth, London. He was the son of Alexander Grant and his wife Marion (*née* Stirling). After leaving the College Grant was employed as a clerk in London. In 1906 he married Florence Mabel Schilling and they subsequently had at least one daughter, Dorothy. In 1911 the family lived in Warnham, Surrey, although they later moved to Dulwich, London.

On the outbreak of war Grant continued to work as a clerk but on or around 8 July 1915 he received a short service commission in the 8th Battalion, Royal West Kent Regiment, and was later promoted to Captain. The circumstances of his death are unclear and it is possible that he died in the Spanish flu epidemic after the war rather than as result of wounds sustained in action in the war's closing stages.

Grant's grave is in the Paddington Old Cemetery, Kilburn, London.

Major Sidney Martin Pearce (School House 1906–1907)

Died of pneumonia, Great Britain, 6 December 1918 (aged 28)

Sidney Martin Pearce was born in Leicester on 6 December 1890. He was the younger son of Edwin Pearce, a builders' supplier who went bankrupt in 1911, and his wife Laura (*née* Payne). The family lived in Leicester. It is not clear why Pearce and his brother were educated at the College and there are few records of their time there. After Pearce left the College he joined his father's business. However, after his father encountered financial difficulties and moved to Lancashire in 1911 Pearce entered RMC Sandhurst and later received a commission in the Leicestershire Regiment.

Opposite: *The Sons of William Parkinson (Captain William Haviland Parkinson, 1891–1976 and Captain Gilbert Maurice Parkinson, 1896–1918) by Maurice Greiffenhagen (1862–1931).*

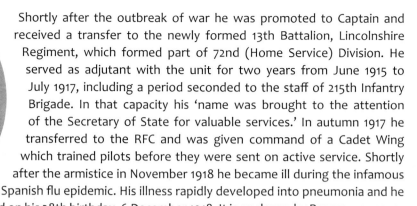

Shortly after the outbreak of war he was promoted to Captain and received a transfer to the newly formed 13th Battalion, Lincolnshire Regiment, which formed part of 72nd (Home Service) Division. He served as adjutant with the unit for two years from June 1915 to July 1917, including a period seconded to the staff of 215th Infantry Brigade. In that capacity his 'name was brought to the attention of the Secretary of State for valuable services.' In autumn 1917 he transferred to the RFC and was given command of a Cadet Wing which trained pilots before they were sent on active service. Shortly after the armistice in November 1918 he became ill during the infamous Spanish flu epidemic. His illness rapidly developed into pneumonia and he died on his 28th birthday, 6 December 1918. It is unclear why Pearce was never attached to a combat unit abroad, which would seem likely given his age and experience but it may be that he was afflicted by ill health throughout his military career.

Pearce's grave is in the Winchelsea Churchyard, Kent, England.

Brigadier General Sir Godfrey Vignoles Thomas Bt CB CBE DSO (1868–1871)

Died of exhaustion, Great Britain, 17 February 1919 (aged 62)

Godfrey Thomas was born on 27 March 1856 in Ceredigion, Wales, although the family seat was in Essex. He was the elder son and second child of Sir Godfrey Thomas Bt and his wife Emily (*née*

Chambers). He succeeded to his father's baronetcy at the age of five and the family subsequently moved to Brighton where he was a day pupil at the College. He completed his education at RMA Woolwich and received a commission in the Royal Horse Artillery in 1875. In 1887 he married Mary Oppenheim, by whom he had one son, Godfrey, who was later to be the assistant private secretary to Edward VIII during the abdication crisis. Thomas served in the Second

Top: *Major Sidney Martin Pearce.*

Above: *The grave of Sir Godfrey Vignoles Thomas, 9th Baronet of Wenvoe.*

Opposite upper: *Portrait of John Burstall.*

Opposite bottom: *John Burstall (back row, sixth from left), at School House, 1892.*

Afghan War (1878–1880) and the Anglo-Egyptian War (1884) and was promoted to Major in 1892. During the Boer War he was twice mentioned in despatches and promoted to Colonel. Following the Boer War he was awarded the DSO and made a Companion of the Order of the Bath. In 1909 he received his final promotion, to Brigadier-General, and was given command of 3rd Division Artillery before retiring from the army in 1911.

However, on the outbreak of war in 1914 he was recalled and given command first of 24th Division artillery from 1914 to 1915 and later of the 2nd Reserve Brigade RFA, a home service formation used for training. In 1916 he was made a Commander of the Order of the British Empire in recognition of his long service. Shortly after the end of the war, on 17 February 1919, he died from exhaustion brought on by his war service.

Thomas's grave is in St Mary and St Hugh's Churchyard, Harlow, Essex.

Captain John Burstall
(School House 1891–1893)

Died of wounds, France, 12 April 1919 (aged 42)

John Burstall was born in Sydenham, Kent, on 24 November 1876. He was the eldest son of Edgar Burstall, a corn merchant who died in 1886, and his wife Hannah (*née* Case). After attending the College Burstall followed his father into the corn trade, joining a partnership based at 34 Mark Lane, London, which traded on the London Corn Exchange, on the same street. In September 1899 Burstall married Agnes Redford; the couple moved to Wimbledon and had six children in total. In 1907 Burstall resigned his partnership and moved with his wife and family to Norfolk where he became a farmer.

After the outbreak of war Burstall volunteered for service and on 23 April 1915 he received a commission in the RASC, being later promoted to Captain. After serving on the Western Front throughout the war he was involved in the clean-up operation following the war's conclusion. However, he suffered complications following wounds sustained on active service and died on 12 April 1919.

Burstall's grave is in Terlincthun British Cemetery, France.

Corporal Christopher Lee Trafford (Hampden House 1910–1916)

Died of tuberculosis, Great Britain, 14 September 1919 (aged 19)

Christopher Trafford was born on 13 December 1899 in Tarvin, Cheshire. He was the only son and eldest child of Alfred Trafford, a bank manager, and his wife Edith (*née* Richmond). The family moved to Brighton in 1911 when Alfred Trafford was appointed to a post in a bank there. While Trafford received a French effort prize, he appears, unusually, to have participated in little or no sport.

After leaving the College, Trafford worked briefly as a bank clerk before enlisting in the Army Pay Corps in which he was based in Warwickshire and rose to the rank of Corporal. It appears from his medical records that he contracted tuberculosis in October 1918 but that he also suffered from tachycardia (an abnormal heart rate), which may account for his not playing sport at school and his purely office-based role within the army. As his tuberculosis had worsened he was invalided out of the army on 21 May 1919 and subsequently died on 14 September 1919.

Unfortunately, the location of Trafford's grave is unknown because he was not officially a member of the armed forces when he died.

Lieutenant Samuel Thomas Newton (Chichester House 1912–1915)

Died of wounds, Great Britain, 13 December 1919 (aged 22)

Samuel Newton was born on 7 January 1897 in Worcestershire. He was the younger son and third child of Samuel Newton, a builders' merchant, and his wife Mercy. While Newton was a pupil at the College he played for the football 1st XI and ran a school record of 23¼ seconds in the 220 yards flat race.

In Easter 1915 he left Brighton College and two months later received a commission in the South Staffordshire Regiment. He was subsequently transferred to the Machine Gun Corps and served in Egypt before going to France in January 1916. On 10 August 1916 he was in a dugout in the front line when a shrapnel shell burst very close to him and he sustained life-threatening, and life-changing injuries to the lungs and back. In September 1916 he was invalided back to the Alexander and Empire Hospital in London from which he was sent home in January 1917 having partially recovered but being paralysed from the waist down. In March 1918 he recognised that his injuries were permanent and resigned his commission. During the next two years, according to reports, he remained of a 'bright and cheery disposition' despite these injuries but unfortunately his overall health was slowly deteriorating and on 13 December 1919 he died quietly in his sleep.

Newton's grave is in Stourbridge Cemetery, Worcestershire. It was recognised that his death was as a result of war wounds and full military honours were granted at his funeral.

Lieutenant Hector Crosley (Hampden 1900–1904)

Died of malaria and tuberculosis contracted during military service, Portugal, 13 August 1921 (aged 33)

Hector Crosley was born in Purley, Surrey, on 2 July 1888. He was the eldest son of John Crosley, a stockbroker, and his wife Mary (*née* Candler). While a pupil at the College, Crosley, according to reports sent to the army, 'showed promise in the mathematical and scientific subjects'. After completing his education he became a member of the London Stock Exchange.

On the outbreak of war Crosley was initially enlisted in a territorial unit but in February 1915 he received a commission in the East Lancashire Regiment. His initial war service was spent attached to the 10th Battalion East Lancashires in Cameroon where, during the campaign against the German colony there, he became ill with malarial neurasthenia. He was then invalided back to Britain for 16 months and thereafter spent some time serving with military intelligence in the Netherlands, which was a neutral country. In late 1917 he was despatched to the Middle East for further service as an intelligence officer. He avoided being sent to the Western Front because records of medical advice revealed that service in the trenches would be bad for his, already poor, health. Following the end of the war he was diagnosed with tuberculosis and consequently relinquished his commission on 13 August 1919. He spent the next two years in Britain but in early 1921 moved to Madeira because it was thought that the climate there would be better for his lungs. However, they failed to improve and he died there on 13 August 1921.

Crosley is buried in Madeira, Portugal. His family clearly attributed his illness to his war service because there are documents that demonstrate their attempts to gain the exemption from death duties granted to those who died as a result of military service. However, it appears that their appeals were rejected.

Opposite top: *Corporal Christopher Lee Trafford (BCRH).*

Above: *Lieutenant Samuel Thomas Newton (BCRH).*

PTE.
P. VEYRIER-
MONTAGNERES

PTE.
H. HATTON

MAJOR.
W. F. A. STEWART

MAJOR.
R. F. C. KING

Brighton College Roll of Honour, in date order.

www.brightoncollegeremembers.com

MAJOR.
H. G. WATKIN

CAPTAIN
R. GRANT

BRIGADIER
GENERAL
SIR G. V. THOMAS

LIEUT.
H. CROSLEY

REMEMBERING THE 149
YOUNG MEN FROM
BRIGHTON COLLEGE
WHO GAVE THEIR LIVES IN
THE GREAT WAR 1914–1918

ACKNOWLEDGEMENTS

We would like to acknowledge everyone who helped produce this book, with particular thanks to:
Paul Brennan for photographing the grave of Sir Godfrey Vignoles Thomas, 9th Baronet of Wenvoe
Commonwealth Graves Commission
Christ Church, Oxford University
Coutts Bank
Fusiliers Museum of Northumberland
Sarah Garcia for sharing her in-depth knowledge of Nikolai de Plaoutine
The Green Howards Museum for helping us research Cecil King
Hastings History House
The Imperial War Museum
Claire Murray at St Mary's Church, Richmond
King's College London Archive
The National Archives
National Army Museum, London
Chris Reynolds at Hertfordshire Genealogy, for supplying us with an image of Harley Duff
Daniel Shearing, Photographer
The Staffordshire Regiment Museum
St Mary's Church, Kemptown, Brighton
Veterans Affairs Canada
Western Front Association

Relatives of the fallen:
Mark Burstall
Frank Gent
Tim Felton
Mike Felton
David Guyon
Elizabeth Harries
Nancy Garner-Smith Myers
Arthur Price
Jenny Waterfall

Brighton College:
Sam Aldred, Researcher
Simon Ashdown, Librarian
Rebecca Findlay, Development and Alumni Relations Manager
Trevor Harkin, Volunteer Researcher
Joyce Heater, former Archivist
Rosemary Lynch, Volunteer Researcher
Isabella Phillips, Volunteer Researcher
David Pincus, Volunteer Researcher
Karen Scanlon, Volunteer Researcher
Joe Skeaping, Head of History
Simon Smith, Brighton College Common Room 1973–2011
Abigail Wharne, Archivist
Tony Whitestone, Brighton College Common Room 1971–2006

The Archivists at the following schools:
Bedales School
Cheltenham College
Marlborough College
Whitgift School

LEST WE FORGET PROJECT, Brighton College 2014/15

With thanks to our 4th Form Pupils and Families 2014/15:

Mark ADARICH Aldrich
Luca ADEWALE Durnford
Sagar AGRAWAL Leconfield
Chris ALBERTYN Abraham
Christian ALEPPO Durnford
Alice AMESS Williams
Emmie AXELSEN Williams
Zhenna AZIMRAYAT ANDREWS Seldon
Isla BACKHOUSE Fenwick
Archie BALDOCK Abraham
Alex BARBIERI Hampden
Alice BARNES Seldon
Natasha BAYNHAM Chichester
George BIRKELAND Leconfield
Claudia BISHOP Chichester
Askar BIZAK Head's
Sam BREWER Hampden
Dewi BREWSTER-DOHERTY Aldrich
Tomas BRIGGS Head's
Ellis BROWN Aldrich
Heather BURROWS New House
Alexander BUSHELL Leconfield
Maddie CARR Williams
Daisy CHADWICK Williams
Toby CHAMBERS Head's
Emily CHETWOOD Chichester
Joshua CHEUNG Jong Yu Leconfield
Arthur CHING Head's
Marcus CHISHOLM Hampden
Jack CHIU School House
Joelle CHOW Fenwick
Ivo CHRISTIE Aldrich
Elias CLARK Aldrich
Heather CLARK Chichester
Conor CLARKE Head's
Violet CLAY New House
Joseph CLAYSON Leconfield
Woody COOK Leconfield
George COOKE Ryle
Amber COUSINS Chichester
Lillian COX Seldon
Edward CRITCHLEY Hampden
Millie CRITCHLOW Seldon
Luke CULLEN Ryle
Craig CUNNINGHAM Durnford
Charlie D'ARCY Aldrich
Oscar DAVISON School House
Louis DE WARDT Head's
Neill DI LUCIA Head's
Anya DOBSON Seldon
Floyd DOUBTFIRE Hampden
Henry DUNFORD Aldrich
Daniel DUNLOP Durnford
Luc EBENEZER Hampden

George EISMARK Head's
Felix EMBREY Head's
Joe ENGLAND Ryle
Arshiya ESLAMDOUST Ryle
Hannah EVANS Chichester
Sam EXELL Head's
Charles FARTHING Hampden
Sebastian FIELDHOUSE Hampden
Rory GABRIEL Leconfield
Ella GEORGE New House
Lexi GHAZI Seldon
Luke GOOD School House
Annabel GOODMAN New House
Vignesh GOPINATH Aldrich
Orlando GRANT Durnford
Henry GRAVES Abraham
Ombaashi GRECH CATO Durnford
Mara GREENWOOD Williams
Jake GRIEVES Leconfield
Jessica GUY Chichester
Jess HAJI Aldrich
Matthew HALES Durnford
Jack HALL Abraham
Benjamin HAMPEL Aldrich
India HARRIS Williams
Oscar HARVEY Ryle
Raquel HEADLEY Williams
Suki HEALEY Seldon
Alice HEAP Fenwick
Jamie HEAP Abraham
Tom HEAP School House
Yasmin HENDERSON Williams
Kit HEY Aldrich
Alex HICKS School House
Lelia HOAD Seldon
Elizabeth HOLLAMBY New House
Ella HONEY Seldon
Shadman HOSSAIN Ryle
Polly HOWARTH Williams
Henry HOWESON School House
Kristina HUCKSTEPP New House
Connie HUNTER Williams
Oliver HUTCHINGS Head's
Edie IRELAND-MYATT Seldon
Monty JACKSON Aldrich
Sophie JAIN Williams
Marçal JANÉ-HEIDSIEK Durnford
Alice JEFFREY Seldon
Teddy JOHNSON Head's
Teri KEJVALOVA Chichester
James KENT Durnford
Bank KHAMTONWONG Ryle
Dan KIMBER Ryle
Gabby KINGDON-LEACH Fenwick

The Welch family home in Patcham, Surrey	64	Wikicommons
The Basra Memorial in its original location	65	Jeff Elson, Head of Research at the Staffordshire Regiment Museum.
Trench warfare on the Western Front during the First World War	66	Imperial War Museum (Q 70168)
In the distance the British battlecruiser HMS *Indefatigable* sinking after being struck by shells from the German battlecruiser *Von Der Tann* first in 'X' magazine and then once she had limped out of the line she was hit by another salvo on the foredeck, the resulting explosion then destroying her. All but two of *Indefatigable*'s crew of 1,119 were killed in the blast.	71	The rights holder (IWM Q 64302)
Photographic portrait of Leslie Woodroffe from the Marlborough College roll of honour.	72	Marlborough College
George Sutherland Guyon aged 5	74	Reproduced with permission from David Guyon
Guyon's 1916 diary somehow made it back from the battlefield to his family	75	Reproduced with permission from David Guyon
Guyon's last known portrait, his diary open at 1st July, and the 'Kings & Queen's'	75	Reproduced with permission from David Guyon
Imperial War Graves Commission record showing details of Gerald Neame's headstone.	77	Commonwealth Graves Commission
A memorial panel list, which includes Theodore Chalk	78	Commonwealth Graves Commission
Imperial War Graves Commission record showing details of David Gaussen's headstone	84	Commonwealth Graves Commission
Photograph of Robert Gordon Melville Mitchell	89	Tasmanian Archives (NS3216/1/1)
Portrait Photograph of Harold Body.	92	Veteran Affairs Canada.
The battle of Passchendaele, July to November 1917	94	Imperial War Museum (E(AUS) 1220).
Second Lieutenant Alfred Sydney Borlase Schiff. Unit: 1st Battalion, Rifle Brigade. Death: 09 April 1917 Western Front.	101	Imperial War Museum (HU 126232)
Battle of Arras clearing station, April 1917	104	Imperial War Museum (Q6195)
The Hundred Days Offensive, August to November 1918	130	Imperial War Museum (Q 9193)
Portrait photograph of Herman Oxley	146	Coutts Bank
Graves Registration Form, which includes an entry for Arthur Cave	147	Commonwealth Graves Commission
The Cemetery, Etaples, 1919	148	Imperial War Museum (ART 2884)
The Sons of William Parkinson (Captain William Haviland Parkinson, 1891–1976 and Captain Gilbert Maurice Parkinson, 1896–1918) by Maurice Greiffenhagen (1862–1931)	150	The Fusiliers Museum of Northumberland
The grave of Sir Godfrey Vignoles Thomas, 9th Baronet of Wenvoe	152	Paul Brennan
Portrait of John Burstall	153	Reproduced with permission from Mark Burstall